THE POLITICS OF
EARTHQUAKE PREDICTION

The Politics of
Earthquake Prediction

by Richard Stuart Olson

with Bruno Podesta and
Joanne M. Nigg

PRINCETON UNIVERSITY PRESS

PRINCETON, NEW JERSEY

Library of Congress Cataloging-in-Publication Data

Olson, Richard S., 1946–
The politics of earthquake prediction /
by Richard Stuart Olson with Bruno Podesta and Joanne M. Nigg.
p.   cm.
Includes index.
ISBN 0-691-07798-3 (alk. paper)
1. Earthquake prediction—Political aspects.   2. United States—
Foreign relations—Peru.   3. Peru—Foreign relations—United States.
I. Nigg, Joanne M.   II. Podestà, Bruno, 1946–.   III. Title.
QE538.8.036 1989   88-22101   363.3√495—dc19

Research for this book was supported by the National Science
Foundation under Grant CEE-824245. The authors bear sole
responsibility for all statements of fact and interpretation.

This book has been composed in Linotron Palatino

Clothbound editions of Princeton University Press books are printed
on acid-free paper, and binding materials are chosen for strength
and durability. Paperbacks, although satisfactory for personal
collections, are not usually suitable for library rebinding

Printed in the United States of America by Princeton University Press,
Princeton, New Jersey

CONTENTS

PREFACE

The vast majority of physical and natural scientists believe that "politics," however defined, is alien to their enterprise, the pursuit of truth. In fact, however, the complex world of legislative mandates, organizational missions, and program choices has a tremendous impact on the scope, direction, and pace of modern scientific inquiry. The research environment becomes even more problematic when the field in question is on a scientific frontier. Earthquake prediction research is such a frontier.

This book is the political history of one earthquake prediction, the 1976–1981 Brady-Spence earthquake prediction for Lima, Peru, and of the scientists, administrators, and government officials attempting "to do the right thing" in a situation of great uncertainty. It is quite a story, if only because of the detail provided us.

Colleagues who reviewed early drafts of this book expressed shock that so much had been written down and amazement that the material had been turned over to outsiders like ourselves. In truth, that takes some explaining; it is almost a story in itself.

Social scientists usually have to settle for seeing the results of politics and inferring the processes from whatever fragments can be gleaned from interviews and the public record. It is rare, too, for scholars interested in the evolution of science to chronicle a contemporary scientific controversy; the norm is to be granted access to notes, letters, papers, and other material long after all the participants are dead or at least retired.

By nature and training, however, scientists write. They take notes, keep files, and correspond. Even when scientists move into administrative positions, they retain these characteristics. Scientists also tend to express themselves with an unusual degree of candor, and because they understand and appreciate the idea of "research," they are open to requests for materials. Finally, the scientists involved in this controversy were aware that it was somehow historically important, regardless of how it turned out. All these factors guaranteed a written record and at least partial access.

Luck occasionally plays an important part in research, however, and a major break came in 1982, when one of the agencies involved, the U.S. Agency for International Development (USAID), published a fifteen-volume report entitled *Lima Disaster Preparedness*. Prepared by contractors led by Robert Gersony, this mostly technical report contained a volume thirteen entitled *Selected Available Documentation: The Brady Earthquake Prediction*. Sensing the importance of the case and wanting to preserve at least part of the documentary record, Gersony and his colleagues simply reproduced in chronological order documents from USAID–Washington, USAID–Peru, the U.S. Embassy in Lima, and other agencies. Running to several hundred pages, volume thirteen is a treasure of memoranda, letters, reports, and unclassified cables. The entire fifteen-volume report was publicly available until the small number of copies was exhausted.

Constructing a skeletal narrative of the Brady-Spence case from the public record and the report by Gersony et al., we were able to approach the other agencies involved (the U.S. Geological Survey and the U.S. Bureau of Mines especially) and ask such specific questions that we were simply allowed to read all the files—hundreds of pages more—and reproduce what we wished, within reason.

The State Department in general and the cable traffic between Washington and Lima in particular was more problematic. Armed, however, with unclassified cables which contained "REFTEL" lists (references to other cables) and with citations in memos and letters from the files, we used the Freedom of Information Act to request more than a dozen cables. Most were Limited Official Use, but some were Confidential. We had to formally appeal for the restitution of "excised" material in several cables. We were successful in two cases.

When we put all of the material together, the quantity and quality were astounding. We then interviewed most of the key participants. Hindsight, however, so colored their recollections that we used the interview materials simply to round out the documentary record.

Data on the Peruvian side were the most difficult to obtain. In a more informal bureaucratic culture, Peruvian government officials tend toward oral rather than written communication, and access is problematic even for Peruvian scholars. Nonetheless, files on the U.S. side contained numerous Peruvian documents, letters especially, and the lead Peruvian member of our team turned up other reports, documents, and correspondence in the course of interviewing around Lima. Information on the Peruvian side was important not only because they were the "victim society," but also because the decision making became highly interactive between U.S. and Peruvian agencies. Indeed, it was a five-year stimulus-response chain.

We should note that this unusually well documented story—drama, really—crosses several fields and disciplines, and we could use only part of the materials provided us, perhaps five percent. Indeed, our problem was where to *stop* on detail. We hope the reader will agree that we stopped in the right place.

ACKNOWLEDGMENTS

Many people contributed to this project, but we want to note especially the openness and cooperation of Dr. Brian Brady, his colleagues, and the management of the U.S. Bureau of Mines, especially Robert Marovelli and Chishing Wang; Dr. William Spence, his colleagues, and the management of the U.S. Geological Survey, especially Dr. John Filson and Dr. Rob Wesson; Paul Krumpe and the Office of Foreign Disaster Assistance of the Agency for International Development; J. Andrew Purnell and his colleagues at the State Department; and Alberto Giesecke Matto, the key participant on the Peruvian side. A special note of thanks must go to Dr. William Anderson, our program director at the National Science Foundation, who not only encouraged the project at crucial times, but also helped all those concerned to understand what "fair witness" social science research could do when each of the participants had only a piece of the story.

Tracking down all of the pieces, however, required a hard-working international research team. The following individuals contributed greatly to the success of the project: Dr. David Snyder, Zoila Gamero de Tovar, Patricia del Hierro, Monique de los Rios, Professor Marvin Alisky, Julio Kuroiwa, Karl Steinbrugge, Robert Olson, and Germán Alarco. Excellent staff support came from Sara Frischknecht, Marian Buckley, Coralie Rose, and Wendy Stricklin at Arizona State University.

THE POLITICS OF
EARTHQUAKE PREDICTION

ONE

Introduction:
Politics and Science

In his seminal 1962 book *The Structure of Scientific Revolutions*, Thomas Kuhn argued against a simple linear interpretation of scientific progress and gave great attention to "paradigms" and "paradigm shifts."[1] An early reviewer of Kuhn, however, noted that he had used the term "paradigm" in twenty-two apparently different ways. In a subsequent (1970) edition, Kuhn apologized and offered a two-tiered redefinition: A paradigm comprises the basic theoretical tenets, shared beliefs about appropriate models, and common values of a scientific community. A paradigm, however, is also a set of "exemplars." These are model problems with preexisting solutions used to illustrate general laws and to train inductees in the field. The newcomers are then expected to extend and deepen the field and "see [a new] problem as *like* a problem . . . already encountered."[2]

Kuhn's image of a basically conservative and narrow-minded science disturbed scientists and nonscientists alike. As Nathan Reingold noted in 1980: "Kuhn's description of normal science as the norm outraged philosophers and others to whom science was an enterprise forever at the edge of knowledge, undertaken by individuals continually challenging existing concepts. A tradition-bound community was anathema to those believing in scientists as a band of adventurous explorers of the unknown."[3]

Kuhn noted that paradigm shifts did not occur easily. Generations of scientists were often committed to a particular world view, with its attendant set of models and problem-solving techniques. They could be counted upon to resist a new approach which might suddenly render their training and experience obsolete. How a scientific community confronted a potential innovation fascinated Kuhn. Arguing that "there is no area in which more work is so badly needed," he asked a series of key questions: "How does one elect and how is one elected to membership in a particular community, scientific or not? What is the process and what are the stages of socialization to the group? *What does the group collectively see as its goals; what deviations, individual or collective, will it tolerate; and how does it control the impermissible aberration?*"[4] Basically, these are political questions, but scientists are reluctant to admit that politics plays any part in their professional lives. Of course, the appearance of being "apolitical" or "above politics" is itself a very astute political tactic.

Among the relatively few major studies which focus on "the politics of science," the works of Don Price, Robert Gilpin and Christopher Wright, Stuart Blume, W. Henry Lambright, and David Dickson are noteworthy.[5] Nonetheless, the dominant focus in all of these works is some combination of the following: (1) the evolution of science as a public policy issue, (2) the impact of science or the "scientific way of thinking" on government, (3) the ad-

4

ministration of science, especially at the federal level, and (4) the organization of scientific communities to interact with government.

While traces of concern about the internal politics of science can be found in most of these studies, only two works really probe the question that interested Kuhn most: how scientists control challenges to established orthodoxy. A partial attempt was made by science writer Daniel Greenberg in *The Politics of Pure Science*, but the major effort was by Marlan Blissett in *Politics in Science*.[6]

The core of Blissett's book is three sections on (1) the structural characteristics of research, (2) the social parameters of science, and (3) the political process of science, especially "the emergence and resolution of scientific disputes." Blissett argues that a fundamental tension exists within all scientific communities between conformity to a prevailing consensus and "satisfying one's own creative, and possibly deviant, curiosity."[7] Scientific communities are thus miniature social orders designed to control conflict; Blissett defines the politics of science as "a collective method for selecting and perpetuating ('enforcing') consensual patterns of perception and ultimately ordering them into a convincing, intelligible picture (model) of some aspect of the natural world."[8] While the degree of control varies considerably from discipline to discipline, little doubt exists that each scientific community has "an establishment," what Michael Polanyi called "chief Influentials," who determine research priorities, career escalation, publication possibilities, and often funding flows within programs. As Blissett notes, the function of this "restricted leadership of science" is clear. Their job is "to preserve high standards of inquiry by screening out suspect or divergent judgments."[9]

Echoing Kuhn, Blissett makes a special plea for research on how scientific communities handle challenges to orthodoxy:

> Even though the resolution of paradigm conflicts provides an unusual opportunity to see the politics of science from exaggerated dimensions, few, if any, studies have been directed to this end. The techniques of interpersonal adjustment and manipulation surrounding these events must therefore be inferred from sketchy historical accounts. Interestingly, at this level of conflict one can sometimes learn a great deal from unsuccessful challenges to existing paradigms or from the reaction of scientists to theories they regard as distinctly unscientific.[10]

The purpose of this book is to accomplish what Kuhn and Blissett wanted most: a detailed dissection of a major scientific controversy of the modern era. This particular controversy revolves around earthquake prediction, very much on the frontier of current research in geology, geophysics, and seismology.[11] Specifically, the case focuses on a prediction by two U.S. government–employed scientists, Dr. Brian Brady and Dr. William Spence, for a series of great earthquakes to strike Lima, Peru, in the early 1980s. The fact that the prediction, and the underlying theory, were ultimately deemed failures does not diminish the importance of the case. Indeed, it actually matches the Kuhn/Blissett plea for detailed research on defeated challenges and on theories regarded as "distinctly unscientific."

TWO

A Prediction Contained, 1976–1979

Background

Great earthquakes tend to be widely separated in space and time. As a result, their cumulative worldwide effects are underestimated. In fact, however, more than a million people have died as a direct result of earthquakes in the past century. Experts agree that the ability to predict major damaging earthquakes even a few days in advance would reduce casualties by at least fifty percent. Such a capability is on the horizon, although it is not as close as was once thought.

Because of rapidly accumulating knowledge of plate tectonics and indications that major earthquakes offered premonitory signs (such as uplift, foreshocks, radon gas emissions), coupled with some spectacular and well-publicized earthquake prediction successes, especially in the People's Republic of China, the 1970s geoscience community was optimistic that earthquake prediction would soon be a regular scientific achievement. In an attempt to identify and explore the various political, economic, legal, and social ramifications of earthquake prediction, the National Research Council of the National Academy of Sciences convened a Panel on the Public Policy Implications of Earthquake Prediction in April 1974. A year later, this group produced a report entitled *Earthquake Prediction and Public Policy*. The panel reflected the optimism of the time:

> Within the past 5 years, many seismologists have become convinced that a new development is imminent, namely, the *prediction* of earthquakes. By prediction seismologists mean that the place, time, and magnitude of the quake are specified within fairly close limits, with the consequence that accelerated planning to save life and property is possible. Established methods for identifying high-risk areas depend largely on the past incidence of quakes and the mapping of fault structures. The new methods rely primarily on premonitory signs, such as changing physical properties of rocks under stress and surface tilting, that occur in advance of a quake. Prediction capability does not lessen the importance of other approaches to earthquake mitigation, but it adds one potentially telling weapon to the arsenal.[1]

Anticipation of an "imminent" earthquake prediction capability was premature, however. Unfortunately, different fault systems have different earthquake mechanics, and the precursory phenomena are hard to detect and even harder to interpret. Optimism faded in the late 1970s, and a 1978 National Research Council panel reflected more caution, even as it emphasized the societal implications of the (eventual) capability to predict earthquakes: "Geological technology will probably reach a point within the foreseeable future at which scientifically credible earthquake predictions can be made. Constructive use of this new prediction technology will depend to a considerable extent on the accuracy and reliability of our knowledge about how people and organizations will respond to these predictions and warnings. Inadequate attention to the social consequences of using a particular technology may have counterproductive results."[2]

Within the U.S., the United States Geological Survey (USGS) conducts or supports most of the basic geoscience research on earthquakes and earthquake prediction. There was an early (1960s) battle over who would take the lead in earthquake prediction research between USGS and the Environmental Sciences Services Administration (ESSA), which subsequently became the National Oceanic and Atmospheric Administration (NOAA), but USGS emerged the clear victor.[3] The USGS budget for earthquake research grew from a few million dollars in the early 1970s to almost twenty million dollars later in the decade.

The Brady Approach

Between 1974 and 1976, Dr. Brian T. Brady, a research physicist in the Denver center of the United States Bureau of Mines (USBM), which is traditionally competitive with USGS within the Department of the Interior, published a series of four articles in the European scientific journal *Pure and Applied Geophysics*.[4] In these "Theory of Earthquakes" articles, Brady argued that he had observed a structure in rock failure which was equally applicable to laboratory rock breakage, mine failures, and earthquakes. The Brady approach represented an unprecedented combination of geophysics, microphysics, and mathematics. Brady argued that his theory yielded a "clock" which provided the precise time, place, and magnitude of an earth-

9

quake, but only if he had the requisite historical and current seismicity data. More specifically, Brady argued that his "scale invariant inclusion theory of failure" isolated three time-dependent classes of earthquake precursors. Properly identified and interpreted, these precursors provided warning of an earthquake ranging initially from a few years, then to a few hours, and ultimately to a few seconds. The Brady model was deterministic in the sense that as the area under scrutiny moved through the precursor classes, the system "locked in" for failure. In effect, the Brady approach eliminated the need for probability estimates, the centerpiece of the conventional approach.

In the culminating article in his series, "Theory of Earthquakes IV: General Implications for Earthquake Prediction," Brady described the application of his theory to five cases: (1) a successful 1975 rockburst prediction in an Idaho mine; (2) a 1969 earthquake in the Soviet Union; (3) the 1971 San Fernando, California, earthquake; (4) a 1973 earthquake in upstate New York; and (5) two 1974 earthquakes near Lima, Peru. With the exception of the Idaho mine rockburst (Brady's specialty), all of the examples were *retroactive* applications of his theory. Within his analysis of the 1974 Peruvian events, however, Brady planted the seeds of an earthquake prediction. He noted that the 1974 earthquakes took place in a "well documented seismic gap that is of a size to suggest that it could have supported a much larger magnitude earthquake sequence than what did actually occur."[5] Moreover, the aftershock sequence was unusually short and sparse, and Brady hypothesized that the November 9 event signaled the creation of the necessary and sufficient conditions for "an impending great earthquake . . . 75 km off the coast of Central Peru."[6] This statement by Brady was based in part on the work of USGS geophysicist Dr. William Spence.

A personal friend of Brady since the early 1970s and an NOAA geophysicist before his unit was absorbed into USGS, William Spence had been a member of a 1974 USGS aftershock study team in Lima. Spence was familiar with Brady's earlier theoretical work and shared with him some of the seismicity data from Peru. In September 1976 Spence convened a meeting on "Global Aspects of Earthquake-Hazard Reduction" for USGS. Held in Denver, the conference attracted the leaders in earthquake studies, and Brady made two presentations which generated "animated discussion."[7] The combination of Brady's theory and Spence's data was the genesis of the 1976 earthquake forecast for Lima that would become known as the "Brady-Spence prediction."

Initial Contacts

The Peruvian government and scientific community were unaware of the 1976 Brady article. No scientist or administrator in Peru remembers any prior contact with, or notification by, Brady. In late 1976, however, Spence sent a reprint of the Brady article to colleagues at the Instituto Geofísico del Peru (IGP) in Lima. The reaction was swift. Understanding the reaction, however, requires an explication of the milieu for scientific inquiry in Peru.

Peru has such a long mining tradition that the discipline of geology is relatively well developed for a Third World country. In 1922, the Carnegie Institute in Washington established the internationally recognized Geophysical Station (Observatory) at Huancayo. In 1947, Carnegie transferred the station to Peruvian hands, and the Peruvian government created the Instituto Geofísico de Huancayo. The first director was Alberto Giesecke, a former Carnegie staff member and of a family long distinguished in the history of Peruvian education.

11

In Peruvian hands, IGP developed slowly and maintained the high reputation of the Huancayo operation. In the International Geophysical Year of 1957, however, IGP entered a period of explosive growth, because the equatorial placement and high prestige of the Huancayo station made IGP the logical recipient of more than fifty international research agreements. With the outside funding, staff grew from four to one hundred professionals.

In October 1968, the government of President Fernando Belaúnde Terry was overthrown by the military under General Juan Velasco Alvarado. This was not a "typical" military coup, however, because the leftist (but still military) Velasco government instituted a series of fundamental societal reforms which (1) broke the economic back of the traditional Peruvian oligarchy, (2) brought large sectors of the economy under state control, (3) mobilized whole classes previously excluded from Peruvian politics, and (4) eventually put the media under government direction. Moreover, the military settled in for extended rule, lasting (with a 1975 bloodless coup by General Francisco Morales Bermúdez) until mid-1980. In truth, the period deserves the term "revolution." That many of the reforms would contribute to economic disaster was not understood at the time.[8]

With the advent of military rule, the halcyon days of an autonomous IGP came to a close. IGP found itself slowly strangled by an expanded state bureaucracy which curtailed its autonomy and by losses in real salaries caused by inflation and a collapsing Peruvian economy.

As 1976 drew to a close, six of the Peruvian scientists with IGP and the Centro Regional de Sismologia para América del Sur (CERESIS) in Lima, which Giesecke also headed, contacted Brady to obtain more information, and one made a point of visiting Brady and Spence during a stop at the Golden, Colorado, offices of USGS in December 1976. Brady has argued that in this manner "the Peruvian government was discreetly made aware of [the] prediction."[9] More formally, Brady began corresponding with Peruvian scientists in January 1977. In this early exchange of letters, Brady was cautious about his forecast. For example, on January 11, 1977, Brady thanked the Peruvian scientists for some historical seismicity data and concluded only that "there are sufficient data at hand suggesting that my conjectures may have some physical basis."[10]

In mid-1977, Spence talked with his USGS superior at Golden, Louis C. Pakiser, about Brady's publications. Pakiser then asked Brady to prepare a background and status report on his work. On August 25, 1977, Brady responded with a technical paper on the 1974 Peruvian earthquakes and a cover letter. By specifying time, place, and magnitude, the cover letter and paper changed the forecast into a *prediction*:

Briefly, I believe a serious situation developed near Lima, Peru, on November 9, 1974. This situation is that the preparation phase for a great earthquake has begun. Supportive data, including recent theoretical studies by myself, suggest that *the magnitude of this event will be approximately M = 8.4 (±0.2) and that the minimum time to the event, measured from November 14, 1974, is approximately 5.9 years. . . .*

I am of the opinion that this prediction has a sound scientific basis and firmly believe that much further study (a portion of which is discussed in the summary) is necessary. The data set at hand clearly indicate that a serious effort to study this region is warranted.[11]

Pakiser forwarded Brady's material to an in-house earthquake prediction panel at the Reston, Virginia, headquarters of USGS. Although Pakiser noted that Brady and Spence had new supportive data not included in the written materials, the Reston group did not respond to Pakiser. The USGS earthquake prediction evaluation group simply did not believe that Brady "was worth bothering about."

In Peru, several journalists obtained copies of the August 1977 Brady document, but the military government prevented publication of any news about it. This policy of suppression would last until late 1979, when the military was about to retreat to the barracks. Although the general public in Peru remained in the dark, Alberto Giesecke kept Minister of Education General José Guabloche fully informed about the prediction starting in 1977, as IGP pertains to that ministry. Giesecke was, however, increasingly disturbed by the dilatory nature of the U.S. government response. Obviously, Giesecke, and indeed all Peruvian officials, saw a more serious problem than did the Americans. At worst, Peru would bear the brunt of a great earthquake. At best, the Peruvians had to be concerned about an eventual news leak and what Giesecke later termed "the potential social and economic implications of such a catastrophic prediction, regardless of its scientific validity."[12]

At Giesecke's request, Pakiser convened a USGS–Golden staff meeting for November 18, 1977, to hear about and discuss "the Brady-Spence prediction." Giesecke was in the U.S. at the time and attended the meeting, out of which came three important documents. The first was a cable from Lima; the second was a USBM memo by Brady; the third was a USGS memo about the November 18 meeting.

Alberto Giesecke had come to the U.S. in November 1977 by invitation of the United States International Communication Agency (USICA), formerly and again presently known as the United States Information Agency.

14

Giesecke attended a "Multi-Regional Project on Science and Technology." According to a USICA–Lima cable sent to Washington, "Dr. Giesecke left Peru with a growing concern about a possible earthquake predicted for the Lima area in 1981."[13] The cable provided background and details on both Brian Brady and the prediction, noting that "given the structural damage to buildings during the October 1974 quake, the event in 1981 could very well flatten the city of Lima."[14] The cable then continued with a report on Giesecke's meeting with scientist Robert Hamilton (USGS–Reston) and on the November 18 meeting in Golden:

> In meetings with Dr. Robert Hamilton, Chief of the Office of Earthquake Studies at the U.S. Geological Survey in Reston, Virginia, Dr. Giesecke explained his concern which was at first dismissed by [Hamilton] calling the theory "far-out." Dr. Giesecke countered with: "If it had been predicted for California, you would not be so casual about calling it far out." The upshot of his Reston visit was that a meeting was called in Golden, Colorado, on the Brady Theory with participants from Menlo Park, California, Golden, Colorado, and Washington, D.C. A panel of scientists and experts questioned Brady about his theory during a hard-driving three-hour session. *The general consensus after the meeting was that the theory was not "far-out" and that there was reasonable scientific basis for its validity.*[15]

The U.S. Side

Also a few months after the November meeting, compelled by the increasing formality and interagency nature of the exchanges, Brady wrote a six-page memo to Robert

15

Marovelli, his USBM superior in Washington. Relations between USBM and USGS within the Department of the Interior had never been warm ("arrogant USGS" or "jealous USBM," depending upon who is talking), and Brady was becoming sensitive to the fact that USBM had no mandate to conduct earthquake prediction research, which was the province of USGS. Brady made a special effort with Marovelli to explain his earthquake prediction activities within the context of his USBM work: "In connection with my ongoing Bureau project 'Predictions and Control of Failures in Mines,' I have found that when certain critical data are available and detected, such as anomalous seismicity patterns, prior to the occurrence of the failure (mainshock), realistic estimates of the magnitude (a measure of the energy released at failure) and the occurrence time of the impending mainshock are possible."[16]

Brady then summarized his publications in the area of rock failure and the retroactive application of his theory to the 1971 earthquake in San Fernando, California, which he argued could have been predicted. Again, Brady sought to place his earthquake prediction work under a USBM mantle: "I am preparing a detailed summary of the rock bursts and San Fernando seismicity data. These data will be included in an article on the energetics of the fracture process in rock. At this time, *I am reasonably convinced that the failure theory developed by the Bureau offers promise for accurate, long-term failure prediction.* The Bureau's record on this subject supports this statement."[17]

Turning to the Peruvian situation, Brady explained his observations about the 1974 earthquakes which led to his "Theory of Earthquakes IV" article. Brady also revealed that he purposely "buried" his prediction: "I suggested in part IV that a potentially great earthquake was in the

16

preparation stage off the coast of central Peru. No precise time or magnitude (except that M > 8) was made in this article, as I had not developed the necessary and sufficient conditions for seismicity precursors. The prediction was also 'buried' in part IV, so as not to cause alarm and subsequent widespread publication by the press."[18]

Brady proceeded by noting that new data and further analysis enabled him to describe more concretely the coming great Peru earthquake. This was the first real specific iteration of the prediction: "*I believe the occurrence time of the forthcoming event will be in late October to November, 1981 and that the magnitude of the mainshock will be in the range 9.2 ± 0.2.* This earthquake will be comparable to the 22 May 1960 Chile earthquake. . . . The Chile event is the largest earthquake to have occurred since the beginning of instrumental seismology (ca. 1900)."[19]

Concluding his memo to Marovelli, Brady isolated the professional dilemma which characterized the entire prepublic phase of this case: Should he attempt to publish the prediction with maximum theoretical and empirical support, or should he continue to allow it to be contained within fairly narrow scientific circles? Obviously, the situation was further complicated by the international nature of the case. Peruvian interests could not be ignored: "Dr. Spence and I plan to write up a detailed summary of these new data and a prediction update in the near future. If possible, we would like to publish these results in the American journal SCIENCE. However, as agreed with Dr. Giesecke at the 18 November 1977 meeting, publication of these new results in SCIENCE or any other suitable journal will be done only in agreement and close cooperation with the Peruvian government."[20]

Although written much later, a memo from four of the USGS–Golden scientists (including Pakiser and Spence) throws more light on the nature and results of the November 1977 meeting. The memo confirms that Giesecke requested the meeting and adds that at least ten USGS scientists attended, the majority from Golden. The summary is especially interesting, however, because it (1) reads rather supportively of Brady and (2) notes that subsequent data analysis "enhanced" Brady's position:

> [At the meeting] *no scientific objections were raised although it was pointed out that Brady's general prediction theory is questioned by some.* It was suggested that recomputing the hypocenters of all relevant earthquakes using a relative relocation method would help to clarify the significance of the seismicity data in the prediction. The relocation of hypocenters has been completed by Spence and Dewey using the joint hypocenter model. *It appears that the seismicity patterns described by Brady as being significant for the prediction have been enhanced by relocation of the hypocenters.*[21]

On May 9, 1978, a regular meeting of the Geological Survey–Bureau of Mines Coordinating Committee took place at the Columbia Plaza offices of USBM in Washington. Robert Marovelli reported on the "Brady prediction" as an "unscheduled item" on the agenda, and the minutes state that a consensus had emerged from the Golden meeting that the Brady theory had a "reasonable scientific basis."[22]

Marovelli was becoming sensitive to the possible consequences of the Brady-Spence prediction, however, because a day later (May 10) his office sent an "urgent" photocopy of a *Christian Science Monitor* article to Brady. The article was entitled "Care Urged in Predicting Earthquakes" and summarized a just-released White House report on earthquake prediction. The article focused on White House Science Advisor Frank Press and included the following quote from the report: "Since a scientific study may have an immediate impact on society, the scientist must show greater concern for what a lay audience might infer from his words than is customarily necessary in the presentation of new or speculative material to a scientific audience."[23]

In Peru

Dealing with the Brady-Spence prediction in Peru was complicated by increasing sensitivity in Lima. In August 1978, Minister of Education General Guabloche asked Giesecke for a written report on the prediction to be passed along to President Morales as well as (1) the foreign minister, (2) the head of the National Planning Institute, and (3) the executive secretary of Civil Defense. As part of the report Giesecke argued for increased IGP funding to be able to map seismicity and possibly detect precursors. The Giesecke position at this time may appear opportunistic, but it certainly had a sound scientific basis: the existing Peruvian seismic detection network was sparse and slow, and a better network would help interpret Peruvian earthquake patterns, including those called for by the Brady-Spence prediction. No special additional funds were allocated at the time, however.

During 1978, IGP forwarded available seismic data and maintained contact with Brady, Spence, and USGS–Golden. As the year passed, however, the Peruvians felt both the ambiguity and the gravity of the situation increasing. Brady maintained confidence in his theory and his prediction, but no major support or attack emerged from either USGS or other elements of the U.S. scientific community. Then, a major 1978 earthquake off the coast of Mexico heightened Peruvian concerns because, in effect, it appeared that the earthquake had been predicted by a University of Texas group.[24] On January 19, 1979, Giesecke wrote to H. William Menard, director of USGS, referring to the successful forecast for Mexico and formally requesting USGS assistance in the evaluation of the "potentially catastrophic earthquake off Peru [which] may be expected in the next few years."[25]

To appreciate Giesecke's concerns, it should be remembered that the history of Peru is marked by catastrophic earthquakes, and earthquake consciousness is part of the culture. Major damaging events occurred in 1586, 1604, 1687, 1746, 1940, and 1970. The 1746 earthquake virtually destroyed Lima and generated a tsunami which came almost a mile inland and killed all but two hundred of the five thousand people living in the port city of Callao. The Brady-Spence prediction was for essentially a repeat of 1746, but larger in magnitude. In 1970, approximately seventy thousand people died in the earthquake which struck northern Peru. Many of the military officers in government posts in 1979 had been through the 1970 earthquake, and Peruvian Civil Defense itself was a 1972 outgrowth of the 1970 disaster.

A recurring problem for the U.S. scientists and administrators dealing with the Brady-Spence prediction was fully appreciating the cultural memory of Peru's traumatic natural disasters. It was possible to intellectually understand and sympathize with Peruvian fears, but the ability to truly *empathize* was inherently limited. Perhaps the best comparison would be to think of the U.S. suffering through a half-dozen Pearl Harbors.

The USGS Response

As a result of the Giesecke letter, Menard asked for a background briefing from Rob Wesson, acting chief of the

Office of Earthquake Studies, USGS–Reston. Wesson's search generated the four-page memo from the USGS–Golden group, part of which was noted above. This memo recapped not only the November 1977 meeting with Giesecke, but also the more than forty years of Peruvian-foreign (especially Peruvian-U.S.) cooperation in seismology. The memo then proposed and justified a USGS–Golden role in the development of the case:

> In summary, USGS seismologists in Golden have had a long and productive working relationship with the Instituto Geofísico del Peru. Moreover, these seismologists have followed the development of Brady's prediction in detail for the last few years. We feel that USGS seismologists in Golden should have a key role in:
>
> 1. Any USGS evaluation of the potential of the earthquake predicted by Brady, including the organization of a meeting where Brady could present the scientific basis of this prediction to a group of critical scientists.
> 2. Any subsequent development of a scientific program to collect field data in Peru that could result in studies of near-field precursory and post-earthquake processes.
> 3. Any development of a scientific program to evaluate the earthquake hazards that could result from the predicted earthquake, due to ground shaking in metropolitan Lima and the surrounding region of northern and central Peru and due to a large tsunami that could be generated by the predicted earthquake.[26]

To understand the purpose of this part of the USGS–Golden memo, it must be noted that in earthquake research, USGS contains three distinct entities: (1) the

USGS headquarters group at Reston, Virginia, (2) the Golden, Colorado, group, and (3) the Menlo Park, California, group. The primary concern of the Reston group is administration and "other than California" research. The Golden group focuses its attentions on worldwide seismic detection and on risk analysis. The USGS–Menlo Park contingent, however, is the USGS "earthquake elite" and does most of the basic research on earthquake mechanics and prediction. Because the Brady approach required so much detection, and because Brady worked only a few miles away in Denver, the prediction offered an irresistible temptation to the Golden group for intra-agency mission enhancement at the possible expense of Menlo Park.

James R. Basley, acting director of USGS, responded to Giesecke on February 1, 1979. Although he expressed USGS willingness "to share the expertise of our staff," he went out of his way to express caution about any ability to evaluate the earthquake prediction: "As you know, the state of knowledge about earthquake prediction is not yet at a level where routine predictions are possible. Indeed, the field is one in which a number of different observational techniques are being developed and in which competing ideas about physical models of the processes leading to earthquakes are being evaluated. No one yet has an accepted method or recipe for earthquake prediction."[27]

The Arena Expands: State and USAID

It was also around this time that the State Department became involved. Encouraged by Brady, Giesecke met with U.S. Ambassador to Peru Harry W. Shlaudeman in late January and asked for help in securing from USBM some of Brady's official work time to continue research on earthquakes in Peru. The assistant secretary of state for

Latin-American affairs, Viron P. Vaky, passed the request along to the USBM director with the reminder that it came from "a country friendly to the U.S."[28] USBM Director Roger Markle agreed that Brady's time could be made available "on an as-needed basis."[29]

Another important actor also become involved in early 1979: Paul Krumpe, science advisor, Office of Foreign Disaster Assistance (OFDA), Agency for International Development. Although he had been passingly familiar with Brady's 1976 article and had talked with Giesecke about Brady's prediction in December 1978, Krumpe was drawn into the case because of the OFDA mandate to respond to disasters around the world. This was logical, for had the earthquake predicted by Brady occurred, it would have been one of the great catastrophes of the century. Krumpe's entry into the case was a turning point, because OFDA is a classic action agency with a mission to promote hazard mitigation and disaster preparedness worldwide. OFDA proved to be a prime mover in the development of the controversy.

Review

With only minor exceptions, the organizational cast for this controversy was complete by early 1979. On the U.S. side were the U.S. Geological Survey, the U.S. Bureau of Mines, the U.S. Embassy in Lima, the State Department, the U.S. Agency for International Development, and the special-focus USAID Office of Foreign Disaster Assistance. On the Peruvian side were the Instituto Geofísico del Peru, Civil Defense, the presidency, and in effect the cabinet structure.

Not to belabor the obvious, but the organizational cast was asymmetrical. On the U.S. side, the prediction had yet (by 1979) to reach the attention level of even the secretary of the interior. On the Peruvian side, however, it already involved President Morales and several members of his cabinet. That is, the prediction was still primarily a "scientific" issue on the U.S. side, but in Peru it was already "societal" and was becoming rapidly political as well. This difference can be explained by two factors: (1) the Peruvian government is smaller and less structurally diversified than its huge U.S. counterpart, and (2) the stakes were much higher in Lima than they were in Washington.

Thomas Kuhn and Marlan Blissett were concerned with scientific paradigm shifts, their substance, and their method of execution. The Brady-Spence case, however, illustrates how difficult it may be to know operationally whether or not a new approach is actually a paradigm challenge. That is, Brady's theory was not so much a revolutionary countertheory as a revolutionary jump *within* a general plate tectonic framework which virtually all scientists accepted. As argued by Spence, who placed a kind of conventional armor around Brady's unconventional assertions, Brady's theory was applicable to certain tectonic environments which consensus indicated possessed catastrophic potential.

The problem for most of the USGS scientists was that while they did not yet themselves possess a reliable method for predicting earthquakes and knew that major advances were necessary, they were certain that the Brady approach was not the sought-after advance. From the majority USGS viewpoint, the Brady approach was too mathematical, too deterministic, and too much a product of microphysics, especially studies of rock breakage. That is, in this instance, the scientific establishment did not possess a fully articulated paradigm, but they had a general idea about what that paradigm would eventually be, and Brady's theory did not fit within this putative paradigm.

Brady himself fell rather neatly into a Kuhnian mold. He was young (thirty-eight at the time of his "Theory of Earthquakes IV"), had been educated *within* the U.S. seismology tradition at MIT (master's degree), but had gone *outside* (Colorado School of Mines) for his doctorate. Moreover, his mine and laboratory work on rock failure (related to, but quite separate from, mainline seismological research) brought him to earthquake prediction *laterally*. Much the same could be said of Spence, who was only a year older than Brady and whose formal education did not focus on plate tectonics or earthquake prediction.

Bureaucratically, Brady was astute enough to portray his earthquake prediction work as a logical extension of his USBM research, and his superiors protected him. Indeed, one USBM official remarked that he rather enjoyed seeing USGS "twitch and jump" trying to respond to the Brady-Spence prediction. As we shall see, however, while USBM could insulate Brady, Spence at USGS was not so fortunate.

USGS was divided internally. The Golden group supported a full examination of Brady's theory and attempted to stake out a lead position in subsequent work with the Peruvians. USGS headquarters in Reston was very skeptical of Brady. To appreciate the Reston position, however, we should remember that Brady was young, worked in the separate field of mine safety, and represented a rival agency, USBM. Moreover, the USGS–*Golden* operation resulted from the absorption into USGS of NOAA scientists when the latter agency was forced into contraction. Therefore, from the USGS perspective, the Brady-Spence prediction had aspects of an unholy alliance. At the very least, the organizational origin tainted the prediction.

THREE

The Stakes Increase, 1979

The May 24, 1979, Meeting

As agreed upon in 1977 and reflecting USGS Acting Director Basley's promise to "share expertise" with Giesecke and his Peruvian colleagues, a May 24, 1979, meeting was scheduled, again at Golden, Colorado. This meeting represented the second major set piece of the Brady-Spence affair and in some ways was even more important than the very public and publicized meetings which would occur in 1980 and 1981. Indeed, the official roster of participants would never be equaled, especially on the Peruvian side. Brady and Spence were present, as well as a USBM official from the Denver office and four scientists from USGS–Golden. Also included, however, were three scientists from the USGS "earthquake elite" at Menlo Park, California, Paul Krumpe of OFDA, and a representative of the Carnegie Institution in Washington. Alberto Giesecke led the delegation from Peru, which featured two other scientists from IGP and a diplomat from the Peruvian Embassy in Washington. The chairman of the session was scientist John Filson, deputy chief of the Office of Earthquake Studies, USGS–Reston.

26

Taking his cue from Basley's February 1 letter to Gie-secke ("no one yet has an accepted method . . . for earth-quake prediction"), Filson carefully avoided any official judgment on the prediction. Indeed, he stated that the purpose of the meeting was to provide technical assistance to the Peruvians, *not* to "endorse, condemn, or otherwise evaluate the validity of any scientific work or technical position."[1]

The session lasted most of the day, and Brady spoke for several hours on his general theory, its retroactive application to the 1971 San Fernando, California, earthquake, and his interpretation of selected Peruvian earthquakes as "precursory" to the coming main event. In the *second* major specific iteration of his prediction, Brady offered the following: (1) a nine-month foreshock sequence of thirteen earthquakes beginning in September 1980; (2) a July 1981 mainshock of magnitude 9.8, rupturing from offshore Lima south to Chile; and (3) an April 1982 aftershock of magnitude 8.7, rupturing north towards Ecuador. Brady noted that the July 1981 mainshock could generate a tsunami twenty meters high, jeopardizing inhabited areas of the Pacific Basin all the way to Japan. For his part, Spence offered analyses of the 1974 Peruvian earthquakes and historical seismicity in the area. In general, he argued for the "plausibility" of Brady's theory.

Most of the criticism directed at Brady during the May 24 meeting came from the USGS–Menlo Park scientists and centered on the lack of an establishing scientific paper. Brady recalled five major areas of USGS criticism. The first four were standard scientific reservations (the theory is difficult; the data could be interpreted in other ways; laboratory rock failures were not real-world earthquakes; the San Fernando data were interesting but perhaps irrelevant), but the fifth demonstrated how overtly political the case was becoming. According to Brady, USGS was worried that if they were to "comment 'officially' or study the prediction and, by doing so, lend credence to Brady's theory, [the USGS] earthquake prediction program will be placed in jeopardy if the earthquake does not occur. One member of the audience then commented that if the earthquake does occur and the USGS had done nothing, members of the USGS may be required to provide details to high level government officials as to why there was *no* response."[2]

Paul Krumpe, the OFDA representative at the May 24 meeting, was the first to note in writing the presence of that classic indicator of paradigm conflict, incomprehensibility. Krumpe summarized the peer response to Brady as follows:

> Complaints were voiced by several USGS participants concerning the difficulty of understanding the theory, defending it and fostering critical debate on it with respect to evaluation, validation and application of the conclusions. A credibility crisis emerged where the USGS geophysicists felt Brady's work may "discredit the scientific method" unless other scientists are able to relate to Dr. Brady's research and evaluate and comment on it. One USGS scientist stated the following: "I don't understand a thing he is saying . . . how can you ask me to join in support of your work?"[3]

Spence wrote the longest memoir of the meeting (nineteen pages, plus six pages of appendices) and directly addressed the paradigm problem:

> Some of the discussion of the 24 May 1979 meeting touched on fundamental philosophical aspects of the nature of the scientific method. Because there is no accepted *physical* paradigm for earthquake prediction, the field has seen a succession of attempts at such paradigms. Because those desiring to predict earth-

quakes do not know exactly what to look for, the field appears to be concerned primarily with a broad range of data collection and hypothesis testing. So it is natural that a precise prediction that is based on a particular one of the available physical theories be dealt with in a very conservative manner.[4]

In a follow-up proposal to USGS–Reston, to which he never received a reply, a USGS–Golden scientist echoed Spence and argued for extensive follow-up work with Brady. He also demonstrated awareness of the general USGS antipathy toward Brady:

> The problem of earthquake prediction is proving to be more complicated than anticipated a few years ago, when the first USGS programs were begun, but the future is still promising. Efforts sponsored by the USGS today, both in-house and through contracts, are exploring a number of potentially relevant areas. Brady's theory is the first to unify most of these efforts. Unfortunately, the USGS has chosen to ignore him at the moment, in part because of the "Not Invented Here" factor. Of course, it is possible that he is wrong, no matter how sound the mathematical approach (an extension of Einstein's theory of general relativity), and no matter how successful the initial "retrodiction" studies have been. However, I believe that this theory is, at best, the ultimate answer, and at worst, the very best starting point for further understanding of the physics of rock failure. The scientific community can not afford to ignore this work any longer.[5]

At the May 24 meeting, Brady made another prediction, or rather a "forecast," this time for southern California. As part of his discussion of the 1971 San Fernando earthquake, Brady argued that the so-called Palmdale

29

Bulge was related to the 1971 San Fernando event and therefore was *not* the forerunner of another earthquake. He indicated, however, that his inclusion theory anticipated a Richter magnitude 6.5–7.0 strike-slip earthquake around the Salton Sea "in the next few years." On October 15, 1979, near the Salton Sea, a magnitude 6.8 earthquake occurred, now called the El Centro earthquake. After the earthquake, Spence sent memos to Rob Wesson and the attendees of the May 24 meeting reminding them of his forecast. There is no record of any official response to Spence on this matter.

Follow-up to the May 24 Meeting

After the May meeting, Alberto Giesecke continued to request suggestions for an instrumentation and research program in order to monitor and interpret Peruvian seismicity in light of Brady's arguments for precursory earthquake patterns. His latest request had been by telephone to Brady and Spence on October 23, 1979.

On October 26, Brady and Spence attempted to respond. Both scientists recognized that there were only "vague procedural guidelines for the transmitting of letters authored jointly by Department of Interior employees in different agencies." Brady and Spence decided to write identical joint letters on USBM and USGS stationery. In their proposed letter, the authors reiterated their confidence in the prediction and added information on Brady's successful El Centro forecast and on independently published findings that major subsidence was occurring on the Peruvian continental shelf—supposedly consistent with Brady's theory. As the authors said in their draft letter:

We are of the opinion that the theoretical arguments presented at the May 24, 1979 meeting, the plausibility arguments also presented there . . . and the "El Centro" forecast and Peruvian subsidence facts move the status of the prediction significantly forward. A critical part of the prediction is a foreshock series to begin about early September 1980. If earthquakes occur that have the properties of the predicted foreshocks, then we feel that the seismological establishment will view the main shock prediction as having enough probability to encourage a thorough search for main shock precursors.[6]

Brady and Spence then went on to outline a monitoring program which included, in order of priority, the following: (1) a major expansion in the number of seismometers, telemetered to a central location; (2) stress gauges to detect large-scale deformation; (3) radon emission tests; (4) geodetic measurements to compare with the data from the stress gauges; and (5) other studies, such as measurement of sea level changes and a search for electromagnetic anomalies. The authors suggested that funding for such an instrumentation net could come from Peru and USAID, especially from Krumpe at OFDA. They closed their joint letter to Giesecke with the following: "Alberto, please rest assured that we wish to help you in whatever way we can. We understand that a prediction such as this is going to be viewed conservatively and, yet, if something constructive is to be done, we have to take certain risks. We would never go out on a professional limb such as we are doing, if we did not objectively conclude that our assessment of the Peruvian situation is a whole lot more right than it is wrong."[7]

Spence sent the draft letter through USGS for approval. Brady did the same through USBM. At about the same time, in an internal OFDA memo referencing the draft of the Brady-Spence correspondence to Giesecke, Paul Krumpe stated emphatically that he had *not* committed OFDA funds for a monitoring program, but had only encouraged properly prepared *proposals*. Significantly, however, Krumpe also apprised his OFDA superiors of Brady's 1979 El Centro forecast:

> Dr. Brady forecast (more than a year in advance) the increased likelihood of an event in the M7 range occurring in the Salton Sea area within a few years. This topic was also presented at the May 24 meeting at Golden, Colorado and was met with extreme skepticism. It appears now that Brady's prognostication should have been closely investigated with a view toward greater understanding of the nucleation mechanism inherent to his inclusion theory. His forecast may well be supported by the seismicity data, in which case significant credibility will be added to the Peru case, although not constituting "a proof" of his theory.[8]

In Lima

Back in Peru at this time, Alberto Giesecke was asked "to make a formal presentation of the situation, at Civil Defense headquarters, to the Vice Ministers and the Directors of all government agencies, including the Red Cross."[9] The purpose of the meeting was (1) to recommend "reasonable" funding to upgrade the IGP seismic detection network, and (2) to assess Civil Defense and general preparedness needs.

Attendees were so numerous at Giesecke's November 9 briefing that news of the prediction had to leak. With the military regime and associated press control then coming to an end in Peru, the media (unlike in 1977) felt free to pursue the story. Between November 10 and November 20, 1979, lead as well as feature stories on the prediction began to appear in the Peruvian print and electronic media. This first stage in the "going public" of the prediction was a watershed. It also sparked a most significant U.S. Embassy–Lima cable.

On January 4, 1980, as news of the Brady-Spence prediction was spreading in Peru, U.S. Ambassador Harry Shlaudeman sent a Confidential cable to the secretary of state in Washington in which he expressed himself candidly. His cable, "The Politics of an Earthquake Prediction," is several pages long and throws interesting light on both the U.S. and the Peruvian policy dilemmas. The summary section, which opened the cable, reflected a variety of concerns:

> The GOP [Government of Peru] has so far maintained silence on the prediction by a USG [United States Government] scientist that a massive earthquake will strike Lima in July of 1981. But word of the prediction has gotten out and the local rumor mill is active. The Peruvian Geophysical Institute proposed a special program to try to verify the prediction by detecting possible precursors but the GOP for the moment has decided to limit its response to intensified Civil Defense preparations. These plans have also leaked and aroused suspicions that the military may have something other than earthquakes in mind. It would probably be best to bring the problem out into the open for responsible public discussion. But how the Peruvian populace would react in that circumstance is difficult to predict and the GOP may calculate that the suspicions and alarm will fade

if the lid is kept on. The USG is involved because of the nationality and affiliation of the predictor. We will have to tread carefully on this one.[10]

Shlaudeman later elaborated on how and possibly why the prediction was receiving attention in Peru:

Word of Dr. Brady's prediction began to leak out when in November it became the subject of serious attention in the upper levels of the GOP. It is not clear why such interest was aroused at that point, but the timing may have been connected to consideration of the budget allotment for Civil Defense activities in the coming year. In any event, Dr. Giesecke was asked to make a presentation to the Council of Ministers last month. The thrust of what he had to say was that Dr. Brady's theory is far from proven but that it is sufficiently serious in scientific terms to call for attempts at verification. Dr. Giesecke proposed a supplementary budget for his institute of 200 million soles (S/251 equals Dol$ U.S.1) to be used in a program of geophysical, geochemical and geodetic measurements to detect the possible precursors of the earthquake as described by Dr. Brady. (The most important of these, a series of foreshocks in September of this year, would require no extra budget to measure.) Dr. Giesecke argued that Peru needs in any case to improve its capacity to detect and measure such activity.[11]

The ambassador then relayed the Peruvian response to Giesecke's proposal and offered additional information and some interesting observations. Approximately ten lines were deleted for national security reasons, and we are left with the following:

After some deliberation, the Council of Ministers decided not to spend the money. Dr. Giesecke was told that the GOP would rely on Civil Defense. He told me that he was disappointed but planned to go back with a more modest proposal. He hopes for some kind of go-ahead from the GOP so as to be able to request special assistance from USG agencies. He continues to insist with what strikes me as unassailable logic that the Peruvian military's concern for national security would be more realistically engaged in his problem than in the "threat" from Chile.

The word is also out that the GOP plans a special effort in Civil Defense. [security deletion] have asked me if I think those plans have to do with earthquakes or something else, such as an attack on Chile, or an effort to bring the population under firmer military control in preparation for a "third phase" of the government of the armed forces.

[security deletion]

Dr. Giesecke in a memorandum of October 2 to the Ministry of Education observed that: "The prediction itself can cause damage comparable to the effects of a large earthquake. The prediction has foreseeable social, economic and political consequences which can develop into a dangerous and chaotic situation—it is therefore urgent that policies be adopted regarding the management of all the information concerning the prediction—the government has the responsibility to inform the public truthfully and to educate the people."

The GOP so far apparently does not agree. The President sidestepped a question about the prediction during his televised meeting with the diplomatic corps on December 31 by responding that there is always the danger of earthquakes in Peru and the country should prepare by emphasizing Civil Defense and employing better construction in its buildings.[12]

Shlaudeman closed with the following:

> I am inclined to agree with Dr. Giesecke that it would probably be best to get all this out into the open for responsible public discussion. I have encouraged him to pursue this aspect of the problem with the GOP. But I can understand the reluctance in the latter quarter. The rumors and fears of catastrophe or sinister plots may fade—at least until September is closer on us—if the lid is kept on and if, as I suspect will be the case, the Civil Defense effort proves to be more talk than action.
>
> In any event, the subject is one that will require our close attention and discreet handling in the months ahead. Because of Dr. Brady's nationality and affiliation, the USG is very much involved. The best we can hope for is a nice sharp little shake here ASAP. According to Dr. Brady's theory, seismic activity in this zone will be "quiet" until next September.[13]

In Washington

On the U.S. side, as knowledge spread through the agencies involved that the prediction was going public in Peru, interagency relations became increasingly strained, and the exchanges took on a more formal, self-protecting, bureaucratic tone. To illustrate, on January 8, 1980, Rob Wesson, chief of the Office of Earthquake Studies at USGS–Reston, wrote to Krumpe's superior at OFDA,

W. R. Dalton, "to set down for you our position on the Peru prediction and the issues revolving around it." Wesson wanted to "clearly state that the USGS does not endorse Dr. Brady's prediction" and emphasized that "setting aside the question of Government policy toward predicting natural disasters in foreign countries, my office cannot endorse Dr. Brady's prediction because he has yet to write down, for comprehensive study and review, the theoretical basis and interpretative procedure he uses to make his prediction. This is a major point that seems to be lost on several of the people involved."[14]

Wesson also informed Dalton that he (Wesson) had *stopped the USGS version of the Brady-Spence joint October 26 letter to Giesecke* on both scientific and socioeconomic grounds: "In my opinion this letter would imply an endorsement of Dr. Brady's prediction, an endorsement that cannot presently be justified on scientific grounds and may not be appropriate considering the social and economic effects such a prediction might have on Peru."[15]

On January 15, Dalton responded to Wesson, and his letter clearly illustrated the problems of the nonscientist caught in a complex scientific controversy: "It is not our intent to promulgate or attempt to lend credence to Dr. Brady's theory. We sincerely hope that his conclusions are in error. *Because we have been offered no scientific evidence to refute his hypothesis, and because of the potential for human suffering if it should be borne out, OFDA would be remiss if we did not remain open to more definitive evidence, pro or con.*" Dalton also hinted that OFDA was about to take the initiative in this case: "*Toward this end, we may request that the principal proponent and those who may refute Dr. Brady's theory meet with me in an attempt to define a rational approach to resolving the dilemma in which we all find ourselves.*"[16] It may be a subtle point, but the fact that OFDA was looking for a *refutation* of the Brady hypothesis was critical. In essence, OFDA was placing the burden of proof on the scientific establishment in general and USGS in particular. Rather than requiring the insurgent Brady to prove himself right, OFDA wanted USGS to prove Brady wrong. This question of the burden of proof would be a constant source of conflict between OFDA and USGS.

On February 22, 1980, referencing both the Krumpe and the Wesson letters, Robert Marovelli at USBM wrote to Dalton in order to clarify "the official position of the U.S. Bureau of Mines." This very complex letter contained multiple messages: (1) USBM defined the earthquake prediction research by Brady as a "personal interest," but (2) USBM held Brady's theory to be a "logical extension" of USBM research, but (3) USBM agreed not to "endorse" the prediction, but (4) USBM offered to make available "a segment of [Brady's] official working time to assist the Peruvian government." Marovelli also informed Dalton that "in concert with USGS, [USBM] *has not forwarded the joint letter* . . . by Dr. Brady and Dr. W. Spence of USGS to Dr. A. Giesecke of Peru."[17] That is, the USBM position was classically bureaucratic. It protected Brady but without committing the organization and thereby maintained formally correct relations with OFDA, State, and USGS.

In Lima

As the Brady-Spence controversy became more public, news leaks and resulting irritations were causing problems in Lima itself. On January 20, 1980, an angry Alberto Giesecke wrote to an old acquaintance at USGS–Golden to point out that several USGS documents had fallen into the hands of the media. The English is a bit faulty, but the message is clear:

I enclose copy of the information which is in the hands of the press and many others. This is not a copy of any document in my files and apparently it has been obtained through a channel other than IGP from USGS. I certainly have never seen this document before. As you can understand, we are quite embarrassed. We have been handling this whole affair with reservation and at the proper government level and at the same time such key information as that enclosed is being made available by some other means to irresponsible people who are using this for political purposes and also to create panic and unrest. If this information were to motivate the government to providing funds for a program of observations it would be fine but unfortunately all this does is to lower the credibility of the prediction. A memo from Brian to L. C. Pakiser has also been translated and reproduced in the newspapers. This memo is rather old but the date has been deleted in the publication to make it look as if this is the latest information. I hope you can take action to try to find the source of this.[18]

This letter, or at least the part of it where Giesecke stated that the leak would be acceptable if it "were to motivate the government to providing funds for a program of observations," raised doubts in USGS that Giesecke had only scientific concerns in pursuing the Brady-Spence prediction.

Review

Kuhn and Blissett wanted to know how a modern scientific community controls "an impermissible aberration."

From the narrative so far, it appears that studied neglect is the first response, but that this changes radically if the bureaucratic arena expands to include *nonscientist* players or if the *media* become involved. The former means a much more complex and formal set of interactions, and the latter raises the potential stakes of the game. Therefore, given that organizational reputations and interests are becoming increasingly salient considerations in this case, let us review where each of the principal agencies stood, and why. We can start with OFDA, which joined the fray only late in 1979.

OFDA was in a terrible position. Brady, and to a lesser degree Spence, could not be dismissed as quacks. The degrees, credentials, and positions were all there and could hardly be ignored. Moreover, everyone knew that earthquake prediction was on the horizon, but no one knew who would, or who would not, make the big breakthrough. Perhaps it would be Brady, who was very sure of himself. Complicating the problem for OFDA was USGS, the agency specifically charged with U.S. earthquake prediction research. For a classic action agency like OFDA, USGS' saying that Brady was "unconvincing" rather than clearly and demonstrably wrong was not overly helpful. For OFDA, the policy, program, and budget implications of a spectacular U.S. earthquake prediction success were too great. Given "friendly" U.S. competition with the Russians, Chinese, and Japanese in this area, Brady's theory could be an earthquake prediction equivalent to the space program's Apollo moon shot. Finally, we must consider the mission of OFDA—helping other countries cope with disaster. Inherent in Brady's prediction was one of the greatest disasters of the twentieth century, the virtual destruction of a capital city of five million people. For OFDA, the Brady-Spence prediction was not merely a scientific question. The prediction cut right to the heart of their organizational responsibilities, and they had to look at the situation in that light. The prediction represented a "mission opportunity."

For their part, the USBM leadership was in a no-lose situation. One of their bright young scientists had intruded onto USGS turf, but he had done so as a direct theoretical outgrowth of his USBM research. It would be detrimental to USBM morale and reputation if they disavowed Brady. Moreover, if Brady proved correct, great credit would redound to USBM for employing and supporting a scientist who had made a significant contribution to humankind. On the other hand, if Brady proved wrong, USBM lost nothing, for earthquake prediction was not part of their mission anyway.

The situation was most bitter for USGS. A research agency which selected its administrators from within its own scientific ranks, USGS was in a real quandary. Brady had described his *prediction* in detail, but the exact nature of the theory-model-equations which yielded the prediction was much less clear. Moreover, Brady had placed his prediction within a plausible tectonic argument provided by Spence, a USGS employee using the Survey's own approach, techniques, and data. It was difficult to attack Brady without harming Spence, who was well liked personally. This problem was exacerbated by internal divisions within USGS. Several members of the Golden group exhibited real support for Brady, in part because they believed that he "might be onto something," as one said, in part because they saw potential advantage for Golden in their competition with the more privileged Menlo Park operation. USGS–Menlo Park saw nothing to be gained from association with Brady and stayed as aloof as possible. USGS headquarters in Reston was obviously closer

41

to the Menlo Park position, but relations with OFDA, USBM, USAID, and the State Department required that they pay at least some attention to Brady.

Finally, as scientists themselves, the USGS – Reston leadership knew better than anyone that earthquake prediction was primitive and that a scientific leap forward was possible. As bureaucrats, they might want to quash this upstart from a rival, poor-cousin agency, but as scientists without a prediction system of their own, they had to keep their minds at least partially open.

FOUR

Bureaucratic Politics
Takes Over, 1980

In Lima

The Brady-Spence prediction went public in Peru at an especially problematic time. Not only was the economy mired in a deep recession, but also the first presidential election in seventeen years was scheduled for May 18, 1980. The election was designed to return Peru to civilian rule.

After the November 9, 1979, briefing by Alberto Giesecke, the Peruvian Red Cross matched hypothetical needs against available resources. Not surprisingly, they discovered that they needed almost everything. In light of the Brady-Spence prediction, the Peruvian Red Cross issued an international appeal for aid. The list included everything from food to hospitals to vehicles.

As part of the overall effort, in early February 1980, Peruvian Red Cross President Juan Garland came to Washington to meet with the new OFDA director, Joseph A. Mitchell. The focus was the Brady-Spence prediction. A representative of the Federal Emergency Management

Agency (FEMA) was asked to attend the meeting, and according to an internal FEMA memo of February 13, 1980, Garland admitted that "while the [Peruvian] government denies the prediction, it also takes it seriously. . . . [I]n private, planning is underway to meet the very specific earthquake which was predicted."[1] The memo also related that Japan had sent a "six member seismology commission to Peru to study the issue," and the team had submitted a Top Secret report to the president and the minister of the interior of Peru. Interestingly, the memo related that "press leaks indicate that the Commission agreed with Dr. Brady and recommended immediate preparatory action."[2]

An incident related to the Garland visit to Washington and the appeal for aid demonstrates how something as apparently delimited as an earthquake prediction never exists in a vacuum. As the military began to show increasing political fatigue in 1980, the "civilian alternative" evinced impatience and a certain spirit of revenge after twelve years of military rule. Unknown hands leaked the specifics of the Garland appeal for aid, and of all the items listed, the sensation-oriented Lima newspapers fastened on the request for 100,000 "body bags." Garland was publicly embarrassed. Why Garland, the president of the Peruvian Red Cross? It turns out that before assuming that relatively uncontroversial post, Garland was the private secretary of General Juan Velasco Alvarado during his presidency.

Also in February 1980, Alberto Giesecke was invited by President Morales Bermúdez to brief him and his cabinet on "the Brady problem." Giesecke has stated that the results of his February 19 presentation were (1) to charge the Executive Secretariat of National Defense [a Peruvian National Security Council], under General Ramón Miranda Ampuero, with management of the response to the

Brady prediction; (2) to commit the government, in the national interest, to a long-term plan for the development of an earthquake prediction capability; and consequently (3) to obtain for IGP a supplemental budget to initiate "a program of activities directed to earthquake prediction."[3]

It is worth noting that management of the prediction was moved up from Civil Defense to *National Defense*, which oversees foreign, internal, and civil defense operations. It is also clear that Giesecke convinced the president and the cabinet that *earthquake prediction* was an achievable Peruvian goal. A few days after the briefing, Giesecke received news that IGP had been allocated a special budget of $1 million (U.S.). Civil Defense was being given $1.5 million (U.S.) to support a multiagency preparedness effort called "Proyecto Alfa Centauro." In a classic move for a Third World government with a constant budget crisis, however, the Morales administration performed a "now you see it, now you don't" maneuver on IGP: they authorized an IGP draw of about $300,000 (U.S.) in March 1980 but told Giesecke to explore aid from foreign governments for IGP "before requesting from the Treasury the remaining two thirds."[4]

General Miranda Ampuero called the directors of the major print dailies and television stations in Lima, trying to convince them to "reduce tension" by downplaying the Brady-Spence prediction. He also urged Peruvian Civil Defense to reduce its emergency simulations "so as not to generate more tension among the populace."

The U.S. Embassy in Lima began to report regularly to Washington on the increasing concern and controversy generated by the prediction. The Embassy also put the prediction in the larger context of the impending change of regime from military dictatorship to civilian rule. In a Limited Official Use cable ("Lima 1782") of February 29, 1980, the Embassy reported that "[o]n Feb 11, 1980, both

Caretas and *Oiga* weekly magazines carried cover stories on Brady's prediction. *Caretas* gave the background on Brady's theory, noting that in Nov 1979 the Peruvian Civil Defense system had Giesecke provide secret briefing to Directors of various Peruvian Ministries. However, news of the briefings leaked and gave rise to rumor of an imminent tidal wave in Lima's Port of Callao."[5]

Lima 1782 also relayed that on February 20, a Lima paper had published an article "extremely critical of Brady, characterizing him as unqualified publicity seeker whose unfounded theories have caused panic, decreased land values and decreased investment in areas which would be affected by major quake. *El Tiempo*, which is opposed to the current military regime in Peru, also charged that the GOP [Government of Peru] was using 'earthquake scare' in order to suspend the ongoing poli process, i.e., scheduled elections and transfer of power to civilian government."[6]

Later in this five-page cable, the U.S. Embassy relayed that Ambassador Shlaudeman had been visited recently by the head of Peruvian Civil Defense, Colonel Heráclio Fernández Péndola. The purpose of the visit was "to reestablish contact between his organization and the Civil Defense authorities of California, as a result of the earthquake prediction."[7]

In Washington

Back in the U.S., Brady had obtained a copy of Wesson's pointedly negative January 8 letter to Dalton. In March, Brady decided to write to Wesson directly, in part to update his prediction, in part to take issue with Wesson. In this letter, Brady reiterated his prediction, but again he altered the all-important dates. Brady was careful, however, to point out that if certain foreshocks failed to materialize, his prediction should be withdrawn:

The status of the prediction is as follows. A foreshock series will commence in mid-September 1980. The time duration of this series will be approximately 328 days. There will be a total of twelve-to-thirteen foreshocks which will be temporally distributed in two active phases, each of whose time durations will be approximately 109 days. The foreshock series will terminate on July 30, 1981, with the occurrence of the mainshock (M ≥ 9.8). . . . This event will eliminate the largest generally recognized seismic gaps in the world, e.g., the inferred rupture zones of the 1868 and 1877 great earthquakes. The event will be followed by a vigorous after shock series. My current interpretation of the spacetime seismicity patterns in central Peru also leads me to hypothesize that a second event (M ≃ 8.8) will nucleate 276 days later (ca May 2, 1982). . . . I cannot make more precise predictions of the occurrence times of the mainshocks (M ≥ 9.8, M ≃ 8.8) until the initiation times of their respective foreshock series are known. I cannot overemphasize that the occurrence of the foreshock phases are necessary and sufficient for the occurrence of the predicted mainshocks. *If the foreshocks do not occur, the prediction is invalid.*[8]

As hinted at by Dalton in January, OFDA moved to center stage during the early months of 1980. More specifically, OFDA convened a multiagency (USGS, USBM, USAID, State, National Bureau of Standards, National Science Foundation, FEMA) meeting to discuss the Brady prediction and appropriate U.S. contingency planning.

Dalton himself chaired the March 18 meeting and later summarized his position for OFDA Director Joseph

Mitchell. Although Dalton considered the predicted earthquakes "improbable," he believed that the U.S. government could not ignore the prediction, "considering the credentials of the responsible scientist." Consequently, Dalton announced the formation of an "ad hoc task force to perform disaster contingency planning for the west coast of South America and the Pacific Basin." Because the Brady prediction was becoming so sensitive, Dalton stressed that the whole topic "should for the time being remain classified (i.e., OFFICIAL USE ONLY)."[9]

A classic example of perceptual divergence also came out of the March 18 meeting. At the meeting, John Filson (USGS–Reston) attempted to cast doubt on the theory underlying the Brady-Spence prediction, but the USBM representatives (Robert Marovelli and Chi-shing Wang) interpreted his comments differently. Wang prepared the memoir: "Filson, USGS: the USGS cannot endorse Brady's prediction because his prediction theory is too difficult to be understood by USGS scientists."[10] That is, apparently not only does where you stand depend upon where you sit, but also what you hear. It is almost as if Filson, Marovelli, and Wang were at different March 18 meetings.

Interestingly, according to the Wang memoir, Marovelli stated at the meeting that "earthquake prediction is not the Bureau of Mines mission." Marovelli also stated, however, that "Brady was allowed to publish his earthquake prediction theory as a part of the Bureau's technology transfer function."[11]

Although the principal result of the March 18 meeting was simply an agreement to meet again, a senior OFDA planner (about to retire) saw need for swift action. In an internal OFDA document, he urged the rapid assembly of experts under the aegis of the National Science Foundation to evaluate the Brady-Spence prediction and issue a definitive statement. As he explained to his superiors (with a rather clumsy double negative): "Without some scientific evaluation which is independent of the work being performed by Brady and Spence, the Peruvians have no reason not to believe that the United States Government supports the prediction. As long as the USGS makes no public statement about the prediction, I believe that the world will perceive government endorsement— since, in fact, Brady is a career scientist working for the government."[12]

This official wanted the evaluation panel to provide preliminary findings within thirty days and come to "a final position within sixty days." One can but wonder how the next year and a half would have differed had these suggestions been adopted and implemented. The fact remains, however, that they were not. No formal evaluation panel would meet until late January 1981.

The Seismic Disaster Preparedness Working Group set up by Dalton met on April 3, 1980. This meeting again reflected the ambivalent desire to "distance" the U.S. government from the prediction while simultaneously taking advantage of it. More specifically, the group concluded that USGS Director Menard should write to White House (Office of Science and Technology Policy) Science Advisor Frank Press stating that the Brady prediction had no official standing. Press would then write a similar letter to Alberto Giesecke in Lima. This correspondence would serve to "separate any proposed planning effort from [the prediction]." At the same time, however, OFDA preparedness planning and studies would go on "until credibility in the prediction and the theory behind it is significantly improved."[13]

On May 6, 1980, as agreed upon in the April 3 meeting, USGS Director Menard sent a formal letter to White House Science Advisor Press. Menard's letter described the prediction and provided a brief chronology of events, including USGS treatment of Brady and his prediction. It ended with what was becoming an official "policy of ambivalence" in which the prediction was used but not endorsed:

> As you may be aware, the Brady prediction has recently been given wide publicity in Peru. Apparently it is also being used by the Office of Foreign Disaster Assistance to provide the focus for a disaster-planning exercise. In our opinion there is no doubt there is a serious threat to lives and property in Peru due to the earthquake hazard. We encourage all efforts that will better prepare the country of Peru to mitigate the hazard of and reduce losses from large earthquakes that will continue to affect that country. However, at this time we do not, indeed we cannot, endorse Dr. Brady's prediction because of a lack of a well-accepted empirical or theoretical basis. Despite our misgivings, however, we are willing to search for any precursory seismicity patterns described by Dr. Brady using the data routinely available from our worldwide epicenter location efforts.[14]

Implementing Menard's promise on May 27, 1980, John Filson at USGS–Reston ordered the National Earthquake Information Service (NEIS) at USGS–Golden to attempt to detect the September foreshock sequence which Brady anticipated. Filson was quite specific in his charge: "Beginning in October 1980, you should submit to me a written report at the end of each month reviewing the detected seismicity in the region of the predicted earthquake sequence. In those reports you should include a statement, based on your best scientific judgment, on whether or not the seismicity is following the pattern predicted by Dr. Brady. This statement should also include an estimate of the uncertainties associated with your evaluation and the uniqueness of the seismicity patterns observed, if any."[15]

The public controversy surrounding the prediction in Peru (but not yet in the U.S.) had made the USBM leadership uneasy. In an apparent coincidence, ABC News wanted to film a "rock-luminescence demonstration" at the USBM Denver Research Center and discuss mine safety implications with Brady. On April 11, 1980, Brady requested permission, which was granted on April 16. On the morning of April 15, however, Robert Marovelli and Donald Rogich (USBM–Washington) set up a telephone conference with Brady in Denver. According to Chi-shing Wang, also a participant in the conference call, the purpose was to make sure "that Brady will not be lured into talking about [the] Peruvian earthquake prediction."[16]

In Lima

At the request of the Peruvian Red Cross and as a direct result of the Brady-Spence prediction and the increasing publicity surrounding it, the United Nations Disaster Relief Co-ordinator (UNDRO) sent a representative to Lima in late May 1980. On June 10, 1980, this representative filed a report at UNDRO headquarters in Geneva entitled "Earthquake Risk and Preparedness in Peru, with Special Reference to the Predictions for 1981–1982." It summarized the situation at that time: "The very specific prediction of a major (Richter magnitude 8½) and potentially devastating earthquake at the end of July 1981 off the coast of central and southern Peru, with origin less than 100km from Lima, has given rise to a situation without precedent both at the scientific and the administrative level. Never before has there been a prediction of an

51

earthquake of catastrophic proportions which states so explicitly, and so long in advance, the location, time and size of the expected event."[17]

The author noted that although skepticism was the dominant official response to the prediction, the Peruvian government was allocating funds for scientific equipment and was making special efforts in Civil Defense and with voluntary agencies. All of the activity was explained as "part of a general policy and not directly related to the earthquake prediction."[18] Obviously working with local experts, especially Peruvian earthquake engineer Julio Kuroiwa, the UNDRO representative also laid out a damage scenario for the predicted mainshock:

1. The number of people killed could easily reach 400,000, mostly in coastal Callao and in "tugurios" (old, colonial-style multistory adobe houses in central Lima). Many of those killed would probably be children, as "one sixth of the schools have minimal earthquake resistance."[19]
2. Approximately fifty percent of private dwellings would be lost, as would twenty percent of the schools and ten percent of the industrial buildings.[20] The homeless figure would reach into the millions.
3. A tsunami twenty to thirty meters high would hit the coast within twenty minutes of the earthquake. Fires and landslides were also a possibility.[21]

Given the potential losses and recalling earthquake prediction successes in China, the UNDRO representative argued for an earthquake prediction system: "Even if the service available at the present time is an incomplete and unreliable one, the fact that it will sometimes work to the extent of saving many thousands of lives, combined with the fact that we can expect a gradual improvement in the success rate, may still make it a thoroughly worthwhile investment."[22]

Finally, quoting "a senior seismologist in Peru," the UNDRO representative could not resist a rather pointed barb at Peruvian government priorities: "Not a single life has been lost through war in Peru in the present century, whilst over 65,000 have been lost in earthquake, yet the cost of launching an earthquake prediction programme would be only a quarter of the cost of a single military helicopter."[23]

Meanwhile, Alberto Giesecke wrote to the director of USAID in Lima, Leonard Yaeger. Giesecke explained that he had talked with both Ambassador Shlaudeman and John Filson (USGS–Reston) about obtaining the services of an American expert on earthquake prediction to advise IGP on their "plans for a long range program to detect and evaluate premonitory phenomena to the occurrence of large earthquakes."[24] Giesecke further explained that although the generic earthquake threat to Peru was the reason for "investing in a program designed for earthquake prediction," he could not "ignore the fact that our Government's approval of significant funds to begin such a program . . . was triggered by the Brady prediction."[25] (The American expert ultimately brought to Lima was Dr. Jerry Eaton of the USGS–Menlo Park group.)

The U.S. Embassy in Lima had requested that it be "kept informed" of prediction-related activities in Washington, and OFDA took charge of drafting an unclassified information cable. Sent in mid-July 1980, this cable reviewed the two big multiagency meetings held in Washington and noted that "Peru's initiatives and regional . . . disaster preparedness present a significant opportunity to further develop the methodology and techniques of contingency planning for disasters."[26] The cable also stipulated that all such activities were "specified in OFDA's international disaster assistance mandate."[27] Most interesting, however, is the cable's statement that "the U.S.G. does not have sufficient evidence *either to endorse or refute* the hypothesis at this time."[28] That is, OFDA was clearly taking the lead in policy formation and saw the Brady-Spence prediction as furthering their mission goal: helping foreign governments prepare for disaster. As an action agency, OFDA was unwilling to wait until a scientific consensus could be hammered out.

On July 28, 1980, Fernando Belaúnde Terry, the very man ousted by the military in 1968, took office as president of Peru. He had ridden a populist antimilitary wave through the elections of May 1980. Now, as the military quickly retired from official public life, Belaúnde filled virtually all important posts with civilians. This was no mere change of government; it was a full-scale change of *regime*. Among many other problems, the new Belaúnde administration inherited the increasingly problematic Brady-Spence prediction. Alberto Giesecke has captured the change: "The new Government revoked legislation imposed by the former regime, changed institutional structures and appointed different people to responsible levels of the public administration—a common and understandable pattern of behaviour under the circumstances. This attitude may also explain why some of the new Ministers and Congressmen labelled the military as 'believers' of the earthquake prediction and denounced Brady as an international terrorist."[29]

Coincidentally, the rhythm of the Brady-Spence case began to accelerate significantly. CERESIS in Lima had received United Nations funding for an October 1980 international conference on earthquake threat and prediction to be held in Argentina. Invitations were extended to Brady, Spence, and approximately fifty other individuals. USBM had no foreign travel funds but did allow Brady to travel on his own. At first, the USGS–Reston leadership did not want Spence to attend, but Giesecke prevailed upon the U.S. Embassy in Lima to intervene. What turned out to be incredibly important was that Giesecke invited Brady and Spence not only to present their prediction at the Argentina conference, but also to visit Santiago, Chile, and then *Lima* on their way home. The U.S. Embassy in Lima concurred on both counts:

> Embassy's assistance in encouraging attendance of Dr. Brian Brady and Dr. William Spence at International Seminar on Earthquake Prediction, to be held in San Juan, Argentina, October 20–25, has been requested by Dr. Alberto Giesecke, Chief of the Geophysical Institute of Peru (IGP) and one of the seven organizers of the seminar. Giesecke also extended a formal invitation in the name of the IGP for Brady and Spence to visit Lima for a few days after the seminar. . . .
>
> Giesecke feels strongly that Brady and Spence should have the opportunity to present their hypothesis both to the international seismologists who are to attend the San Juan conference and to Peruvian experts at IGP, and on an exceptional basis the seminar organizers have agreed to pay the travel and per diem of the two men. The Embassy concurs in Dr. Giesecke's view and believes that the visit to Peru would be most useful, coming as it would just during or after the period for which the foreshocks are predicted. Without the foreshocks, Brady and Spence have said, the prediction for the big 1981 earthquake is invalid. . . .
>
> It is requested that the Department advise U.S. Department of Interior, Bureau of Mines and U.S. Geological Survey of the foregoing and encourage

participation of both Brady and Spence at the San Juan conference, as well as stop-over in Lima to talk to IGP enroute back to the U.S.[30]

Ultimately, USBM allowed Brady and USGS allowed Spence to attend the conference, but not as agency representatives.

The next major event in the unfolding of the case was the USAID-funded two-week visit (August 17–September 1, 1980) to Peru by Dr. Jerry Eaton, a USGS–Menlo Park geophysicist. According to Eaton, his trip had several purposes. First, he was to discuss with Alberto Giesecke and General Miranda Ampuero (of the Executive Secretariat of National Defense) the following:

1. the scientific merit of the Brady-Spence prediction,
2. the long-term threat to Peru of major earthquakes in the country,
3. the importance and appropriateness of the earthquake studies program carried out by the Instituto Geofisico del Peru.[31]

Second, Eaton was to discuss the same three topics with Ambassador Shlaudeman and USAID officials at the Embassy. Finally, he was also to examine the IGP field stations and advise on ideas for upgrading IGP seismic detection capabilities. Again showing how sensitive—and bureaucratic—the Brady-Spence prediction was becoming, Eaton wrote a formal trip report which explicitly *avoided* any mention of his first two purposes and concentrated solely on the relatively uncontroversial issue of IGP capabilities and needs. As Eaton explained, "In accordance with recent telephone conversations with Mr. William Rhodes, USAID Washington, this report will address itself primarily to an evaluation of the senior staff, current program, plans for an expanded program, and principal difficulties facing IGP."[32]

The Eaton visit was also the subject of a cable from the U.S. Embassy in Lima to the State Department, with attention to OFDA. This cable indicated that Giesecke and IGP would be seeking USAID/OFDA funding for a variety of projects and technical assistance, but that Giesecke had now expressed a desire to see *OFDA representatives* also attend the Argentina conference and then visit Lima: "Dr. Giesecke proposes that OFDA send representative(s) to the regional seminar on 'Seismic Prediction and Evaluation of the Dangers of Earthquakes' to be held in San Juan, Argentina, October 20–24, 1980. . . . Mission encourages OFDA participation in seminar in San Juan, followed by a short visit to Lima to discuss with Civil Defense the feasibility of holding regional preparedness seminar in Peru."[33]

Meanwhile, as a follow-up to the previous visit, UNDRO official John Tomblin went to Lima for nine days in early October 1980. It was explicitly stated that the Brady-Spence prediction, and reaction to it, were the primary reasons for his trip.[34] Tomblin visited Peruvian Civil Defense, IGP, CERESIS, the Red Cross, the National Engineering University, and relief agencies. From his trip report to UNDRO in Geneva, it appears that his goals included (1) a "needs assessment" to respond to both the prediction and a disaster and (2) a corresponding list of projects which UNDRO or OFDA might support financially. The first suggested item on Tomblin's list was the preparation of "an evacuation plan for central Lima in response to imminent earthquake prediction."[35] The second project idea was a tsunami risk analysis. Other items included a risk analysis in Arequipa (far to the south of Lima), study of the very fragile Lima water system, communications equipment, and consultant services for earthquake and tsunami preparedness and prediction response. That is, virtually every project idea was connected to the Brady-Spence prediction.

The Argentina Conference

There can be little doubt that the CERESIS International Seminar on Earthquake Prediction and Evaluation of Seismic Hazard showcased the Brady-Spence prediction. Not only did their paper, "Hypothesis for the Prediction of the Occurrence of an Earthquake in the Peruvian and Northern Chile Coast," lead off the conference, but also, according to the program, Brady and Spence were the focus of no fewer than six presentations or roundtable discussions by other participants.

Although the USGS–Reston leadership may not have fully anticipated the prominent position given Brady and Spence at San Juan, they certainly had some inkling. A few days before the conference was to open, USGS–Reston drafted a cable for State Department transmission to the U.S. embassies in Lima and Buenos Aires. This Limited Official Use cable, "State 277382," was sent October 17, 1980. The cable opened by informing the Lima and Buenos Aires embassies that USGS–Golden scientist Dr. Sylvester (Ted) Algermissen would be accompanying Spence to Argentina and then to Peru. The key paragraph, however, was a USGS warning that it emphatically did not support the prediction or anything associated with it: "The USGS has a lead role in the United States National Earthquake Hazard Reduction Program and is responsible for the evaluation of predictions of domestic earthquakes. USGS scientists have informally reviewed Dr. Brady's theory and they are skeptical of its validity. *The USGS does not repeat not* endorse Brady's theory or predictions based on it."[36]

State 277382 then extended the negation to cover the entire U.S. government, but it could not escape the other horn of the dilemma, the generic earthquake threat to Peru. As the cable noted: "Embassies should be aware that Brady and Spence speak as scientists and that *the U.S. Government does not repeat not endorse* specific predictions based on their work. There is no doubt that there is a serious threat to lives and property in Peru due to earthquake hazard. We encourage and shall, to the best of our ability, assist in efforts to mitigate the earthquake hazard in Peru and to reduce losses from large earthquakes that will, no doubt, continue to affect that country."[37]

Finally, the cable notified Lima and Buenos Aires that *Algermissen* had been "briefed on this position [rejection of the specific prediction but acknowledgment of a general threat to Peru] and should be used as a source of further information or scientific advice."[38] That is, Brady and Spence were not appearing as organization representatives, but Algermissen was. As a good scientist, however, Algermissen may not have understood what Reston wanted. He did not go out of his way to attack Brady or Spence in public.

Neither Brady nor Spence remembers any direct attacks on their work at the San Juan meetings. Clarence Allen, chairman of the USGS-organized National Earthquake Prediction Evaluation Council (NEPEC), attended, and even he (according to Brady) listened politely and expressed interest in the prediction. It was also at the Argentine conference that Clarence Allen and Alberto Giesecke discussed for the first time the possibility of a NEPEC review of the Brady-Spence prediction. In fact, however, the Brady-Spence prediction had been on the agenda of NEPEC since its inception. At its organizational meetings in early February 1980, NEPEC addressed the question "how should predictions in foreign countries be treated?" In obvious reference to the Brady-Spence prediction, the minutes reference "discussion of how predictions made in the United States for foreign earthquakes had placed the Federal Government in a sensitive position."[39]

In Lima

After a bus ride over the Andes at the conclusion of the conference and a stopover in Santiago, Chile, Brady and Spence arrived at the Peruvian capital on October 26, 1980. The next few days would fundamentally alter the course of this scientific controversy. As a high U.S. Embassy official in Lima at the time said in a later interview, "all hell broke loose" as a result of those "four days in October."

Brady and Spence were to meet with U.S. Embassy officials, IGP scientists, and Peruvian Civil Defense officers. Alberto Giesecke, however, had also arranged an October 29 meeting with the *president of Peru*, Fernando Belaúnde Terry, at the palace in downtown Lima.

Knowledgeable sources indicate that prior to the meeting, the San Juan conference was portrayed to President Belaúnde as adding "increased credibility" to the Brady-Spence prediction. Details of the October 29 meeting are unattainable, but we do have two general accounts by first-hand observers. The first comes from an internal OFDA document:

> Met with President Belaunde. Giesecke introduced subject by indicating international exposure to the prediction. It has not been endorsed nor denied. Introduced Brian Brady who presented brief overview of theoretical basis and current status of prediction. Bill Spence presented the historical context of pre-

dicted earthquake with respect to regional geotectonics. The President inquired as to possible options. Brady and Spence discussed possible precursor monitoring program. Giesecke placed all within context of IGP proposed earthquake prediction program. The President suggested Civil Defense and public awareness as potential mitigation factors. Lamberty [deputy chief of mission] offered possible U.S. assistance in support of priority initiatives identified by meeting participants. Lamberty suggested quid pro quo Peruvian support. President replied, "We offer the environment." Giesecke was designated Peruvian scientific contact for program development. Following official visit, Lamberty requested Brady, Spence and Algermissen provide list of priority projects regarding above for transmittal to Washington.[40]

The second account is part of another key cable in this case: "Lima 10336," a Limited Official Use seven-page transmission of November 10, 1980, from the U.S. Embassy in Lima to the State Department. Lima 10336 is important not only because it contains a great deal of information, but also because it constituted "an action request." That is, it forced decisions in Washington.

Lima 10336 opened with a recap of the Brady-Spence agenda in Lima and a list of the key participants in the various meetings. It then described the meeting with President Belaúnde:

The possible catastrophic proportions of the forecasted event suggested to all participants that the prudent thing to do would be to bring more resources to bear in the collection, processing and transmission of the seismic data that feeds Brady's model and to the analysis of the model and its output. To this end President Belaunde indicated that he

61

was personally interested in the project and directed Dr. Alberto Giesecke . . . to be the principal on the Peruvian side. . . . It was felt that while there was no incontrovertible evidence that the prediction had validity, this did not mean that it should be ignored. It was noted that Drs. Brady and Spence gave a 2½ hour presentation at a meeting held in San Juan, Argentina, October 20 on the theoretical basis and data support for the predicted Peruvian earthquake. At this international conference on Earthquake Prediction and Seismic Risk Evaluation, we were told by attendees other than Brady and Spence that discussions with others interested in earthquake prediction and tectonics concluded that there was some possibility of the occurrence of this earthquake and that, by all means, it deserved further scrutiny and study.[41]

The cable further reported that IGP seismic data "just made available to Brady and Spence" during their Lima visit "seems to be consistent with the model and confirm its predictions," at least according to Brady. Lima 10336 reported that the Peruvian government was allocating $500,000 (U.S.) for the data collection and analysis project, and then the Embassy made its first action request: $930,000 from USAID or OFDA for a data processing system, seismic detection stations, strain gauges, and other equipment and technical assistance. Lima 10336 added a further note of urgency to the request:

Despite Embassy efforts to avoid publicity, the press has already reported on Brady's prediction and coverage can be expected to intensify. Knowledge of the prediction is growing and will become common among the U.S. official and non-official community. Concern will grow as the doomsday date approaches. USG officials have made the forecast. The GOP is looking to the USG for help and the American community, official and non-official, will eventually demand guidance and assurances that actions are being taken to safeguard them. Unfortunately, without the rapid commencement of the increased monitoring effort proposed, which requires the assistance recommended in this cable, the time lag in determining whether the Brady prediction model is valid is excessive.[42]

Consistent with Lima 10336, OFDA officials Fred Cole and Paul Krumpe filed their own trip report, prepared in Lima at the request of the USAID mission and dated November 7, but they also prepared an internal addendum once they were back in Washington. Dated November 12, their assessment of Peruvian Civil Defense was not reassuring: "It is evident that the specter of a major natural disaster is intimidating. They are loath to admit that a significant disaster relief effort is beyond their grasp and are wary of asking for assistance they know they need. They are conscious of being deficient in preparing the public for an emergency and seem not to know how to get started. There is an aura of inertia which stems the will to proceed with an active preparedness and response program."[43]

The assistance recommendations of Cole and Krumpe fell into two generic categories. The first general recommendation was for "scientific instrumentation and technical assistance," and it was overtly focused on the prediction. The goal was to "immediately implement a program in real-time seismic data collection, reduction and analysis, *concentrating on the inclusion zone, to monitor the hypothesized foreshocks and precursory events*."[44] The second general recommendation was to support a broad upgrading of civil preparedness, very similar to the Tomblin/UNDRO suggestions.

Differing Data Interpretations

A great deal obviously depended on interpretations of seismicity in Peru, and during their visit to Lima, Brady and Spence reviewed the *local* seismicity records for the previous few months. While Brady believed that they conformed to the prediction, Spence did not agree, and in retrospect believed that Brady was "reaching" for the confirmation so long denied him by his peers.

We should contrast Brady's positive interpretation of Peruvian seismicity with the report sent to John Filson at USGS–Reston by the worldwide earthquake detection center. Dated November 3, 1980, it read as follows:

> Summary for September, 1980—only one earthquake was detected by NEIS in the region of interest. . . . This earthquake was detected solely on the basis of data reported from six stations of the Peruvian local network. An examination of the seismogram from our Albuquerque, New Mexico, station revealed no detection for this event, which meant that it was at least less than mb 3.8 (about one millimicron of ground motion at that station). On the basis of this report on detectable seismicity in the region of interest for September, 1980, *we must conclude that the pattern of seismicity predicted by Brady has not commenced.*[45]

This should be contrasted with the Krumpe/Cole memo of November 12 to Alan Van Egmond at OFDA: "The 'Brady Prediction' currently (November 1980) is 'on schedule' (preliminary data suggest seismicity has occurred in the predicted zone) according to Drs. Brady and Spence (following their examination of local seismicity and rock strain data obtained by the regional Peruvian network (IGP). . . . The 'prediction' will be revised by Brady as deterministic 'marker' events occur and establish the sequence, timing and pattern of future events leading to the occurrence of the mainshock."[46]

That is, USGS saw some local data and data from its worldwide detection system as *disconfirming* Brady, while Brady, Krumpe, and, through them, OFDA, saw local IGP and other data as *supporting* the prediction.

Review

Although Brian Brady was making small changes in the timing of the predicted earthquakes, mid-1981 remained the "doomsday" period. Given the media coverage of the prediction in Peru and then in South America generally after the Argentina meetings, it is small wonder that the evolutionary pace of this controversy increased dramatically in 1980.

As the drama will unfold even more quickly in succeeding chapters, it becomes again necessary to pause and assess our story on a variety of fronts. Let us highlight major items from the present chapter:

1. A total regime change from military to civilian government was underway in Peru, and the Brady-Spence prediction became involved in this highly problematic transition. Except for Alberto Giesecke, most of the decision makers who would have to deal with the prediction on the Peruvian side in late 1980 and then in 1981 were new.

2. As press control was lifted in Peru, media coverage—responsible and irresponsible—of the prediction increased. The Brady-Spence prediction was becoming a major *public*, not simply a government or administrative, issue.

3. Formal statements to the contrary, the military and then the civilian government of Peru were very concerned

about the Brady-Spence prediction and its societal implications. Appeals for assistance and United Nations visits
were the external manifestations of this concern, but the
fact that the management of the prediction was *moved up*
from Civil Defense to the Peruvian equivalent of the National Security Council demonstrates how sensitive the
issue was becoming.

4. Alberto Giesecke was increasingly worried as 1980
progressed. A variety of factors explain the concern: (a)
the lead time to the prediction was narrowing; (b) no
clear negative consensus on the underlying theory had
yet emerged; (c) a tremendous opportunity for IGP organizational enhancement—equipment and personnel—was
inherent in the prediction; and (d) Giesecke had better
connections with the civilian Belaúnde government than
he had enjoyed with either of the two preceding military
governments.

5. The emerging "policy of ambivalence" on the U.S.
side reflected a classic bureaucratic compromise. USGS
avoided formal U.S. government endorsement of the prediction; Brady and USBM, however, saw at least recogni-
tion of the generic earthquake threat to Peru and attention to, if not acceptance of, the Brady-Spence prediction.
Interestingly, OFDA's "neutral" stance and policy of ambivalence were to the considerable advantage of Brady,
because they evinced a clear unwillingness to accept the
scientific preeminence of USGS. In fact, a tacit bureau-
cratic/international alliance was developing. On one side
were Brady and USBM with Krumpe and OFDA. On the
other side were Filson, Wesson, and USGS in general,
with the State Department moving into support. Caught
in the middle were IGP, the U.S. Embassy, and the
USAID mission in Peru. The tensions and conflicts between these groupings were to become even more pronounced in late 1980 and then in the climactic 1981.

FIVE

Late 1980: The Prediction
Goes Public—in the U.S.

The Allen Disclosure

Whatever scientific disagreements over data interpretation may have been developing at this time between USGS, USBM, and OFDA, they pale by comparison with what was happening in southern California. The controversy was about to go massively public—*but this time in the U.S.*

After returning to southern California from the Argentina conference, NEPEC Chairman Clarence Allen attended a media reception which started with Voyager briefings at the Jet Propulsion Laboratory and then moved over to Cal Tech for earthquake discussions. According to one of the reporters present, Allen related over dinner stories about the San Juan conference and provided an overview of the "Brady-Spence" prediction. Suddenly, reporters from major dailies and at least one wire service "sat bolt upright and grabbed for their notebooks."[1]

Over the weekend, Brady and Spence were besieged by

telephone calls from various reporters, and they gave extended interviews. Major news stories appeared shortly thereafter around the country, for example: "Scientists Predicting Peru Quake," *Boston Globe*, November 9, 1980; "Great Quakes Predicted for Peru," *Miami Herald*, November 10, 1980; "Huge August Earthquake Predicted for Peru and Chile," *New York Times*, November 16, 1980.

In Allen's defense, it should be noted that the NEPEC chairman believed that the prediction was *already* public because of media exposure in Lima and coverage of the Argentina conference by South American media. As a seismologist, however, he was unaware of the biased filtering of "Third World" news to the U.S. that yielded *no coverage* of the Brady-Spence prediction until Allen mentioned it. As one of the reporters explained, "Earthquake prediction stories from South America are discountable, but Clarence Allen talking about a prediction is news."

To illustrate the filtering process, approximately one dispatch per month on the Brady-Spence prediction had been filed out of UPI–Lima for New York from October 1979 to November 1980. The records at AP–Lima show a few stories filed from October to December 1979 and stories filed every five or six weeks from June 1980 to January 1981. Reuters–Lima filed five earthquake prediction stories in 1979–80. The lack of attention given these filings was explained by a UPI reporter in Lima who said that leading U.S. dailies ask for follow-up or background materials only on (1) coups, (2) expropriations, and (3) elections. Otherwise, little interest is shown.

In Washington

Allen's disclosure charged the environment in which the U.S. government had to formulate a response to action request Lima 10336. Increasingly the lead agency on the Brady-Spence prediction, OFDA convened a multiagency meeting on November 14, 1980. According to an internal OFDA summary of the meeting, almost two dozen people attended, representing at least ten different agencies. Positions were suddenly much "harder." Moreover, the State Department representative related that a classic bureaucratic "miscommunication" had occurred with the Brady-Spence visit to Lima:

> Mr. J. A. Purnell, State Desk Officer, mentioned that he had talked with Ambassador Corr [who had replaced Harry Shlaudeman] earlier in the day and that a "sense of doom" prevailed in the American Community in Lima due to the recent Brady/Spence visit. Purnell questioned how and why the Embassy could have permitted a visit to President Belaunde by the U.S. contingent visiting Lima inasmuch as Brady's prediction is *not* USG endorsed nor sanctioned in any way. Corr was apparently unaware that Brady and Spence were *not* on official travel, rather were funded by CERESIS to visit Peru. . . . Purnell was unaware that [OFDA] specifically informed Embassy staff that Brady/Spence visit was funded by CERESIS and that Brady prediction was not endorsed by the USG.[2]

According to this OFDA document, John Filson (USGS–Reston) repeated his organization's skepticism about the prediction and stated that USGS would not make Spence available to work full time on the Brady prediction because "to do so would constitute a tacit USGS endorsement of the Brady hypothesis."[3] On the other hand, however, the *USBM* representative said that Brady was a "credible, capable, competent scientist" and that USBM would make his time available "if so requested and permitted by USG policy."[4]

In a different internal OFDA report, the chairman of the November 14 meeting, Alan Van Egmond, who had replaced William Dalton in this area, summarized his feelings about the Brady case and recommended a course of action for his agency. Again the idea was to take advantage of the situation but "decouple" it from the prediction: "Obviously, Dr. Brady has touched a very sensitive nerve in the American scientific community. Earthquake prediction is in its infant stages; anyone purporting to be able to predict earthquakes with some accuracy is likely to be regarded as a kook. The problem from OFDA's standpoint is that there is a chance, however slim, that Dr. Brady may be right. Even if he is only half-right, OFDA must exercise its responsibility to help Peru prepare for disasters." Later, Van Egmond argued: "Regardless of whether Dr. Brady's prediction is creditable, there is a consensus that Peru, and the Andean region generally, is ripe for another major earthquake." Finally, he suggested the following: "OFDA's focus therefore should be on assisting the Government of Peru to prepare for the overall threat with no direct linkage to the specific events predicted by Dr. Brady."[5]

It was also at this time, the third week of November, that John Filson called William Spence in Colorado and summoned him to USGS–Reston headquarters "to explain his behavior in Peru." Spence appeared before Director Menard, Filson, and several other senior seismologists. As a result of this meeting, Spence began to feel intense pressure to disassociate himself from Brady.

On November 19, 1980, a small, high-level group meeting took place, the purpose of which was to discuss the whole Peruvian earthquake situation. Gordon Pierson, USAID deputy assistant administrator with oversight responsibilities for OFDA, hosted the group. The others present were Alan Van Egmond (OFDA), Rob Wesson

(USGS–Reston), John Filson (USGS–Reston), and Edward Coy, acting assistant administrator, USAID Bureau for Latin America and the Caribbean.

According to Van Egmond, Pierson opened the meeting by summarizing USAID's intended response to Lima 10336 and related that USAID Administrator Douglas Bennett had talked with White House Science Advisor Frank Press. Subsequently, Bennett had asked Pierson "to ascertain what [the] USGS position was on the Brady Prediction and why thus far USGS has apparently pursued a non-responsive approach."[6] Wesson defended USGS with a long explanation of the "infancy" of earthquake prediction and noted that Brady, a specialist in rock mechanics, had "no standing among U.S. seismologists." Wesson then revealed that USGS had "expressed concern to the U.S. Bureau of Mines about Dr. Brady's persistence in advocating his prediction." Wesson pointed out that USBM had been "rather lenient in allowing Brady to continue his work on this subject, much to the chagrin of USGS."[7]

Van Egmond elaborated on how Wesson and USGS viewed the San Juan conference and the ensuing Brady-Spence stopover in Lima:

> Wesson stated that USGS thought the focus of the conference was on regional seismic programs. Dr. Spence was allowed to attend as a private U.S. citizen with funds paid for by Conference sponsors. The U.S. Bureau of Mines allowed Dr. Brady to attend, apparently on the same basis. The USGS also sent Dr. Ted Algermissen from Denver, Colorado as a "voice of reason." Dr. Allen of Cal Tech also attended the conference.
>
> Subsequently, according to Wesson, the USGS was shocked to learn that much of the attention of the

conference was centered on the Brady prediction. Furthermore, to their horror, Drs. Brady and Spence stopped in Lima, and at Dr. Giesecke's initiative met with the President of Peru.

Wesson related that in USGS' view, they are being leveraged by Dr. Giesecke to provide more assistance to the Peruvian Geophysical Institute (IGP) which he heads. In Wesson's judgment, Dr. Giesecke is a highly capable geophysicist, but has ulterior motives in seeking to expand his program and personal position. Wesson also stated the USGS was very disappointed in Dr. Spence's conduct, who perhaps went beyond reasonable bounds in creating the impression of tacit USG endorsement for the Brady model. Finally, Wesson stated that the Peruvian Government has yet to request USG assistance in evaluating the Brady prediction, nor has Brady set forth his hypothesis in a manner conducive to scientific review and testing.[8]

The remainder of the meeting was given over to discussing proper courses of action, balancing further assistance with avoidance of a tacit U.S. government endorsement of the prediction. According to Van Egmond, the group agreed on the following division of labor:

1. OFDA would be responsible for coordinating the drafting of a cable to Lima in response to Lima 10336.
2. OFDA would be responsible for drafting sections of the cable dealing with risk analysis, preparedness and public awareness. OFDA would also determine whether certain activities sponsored under CERESIS could be accelerated.
3. USGS would be responsible for drafting a section on procedures for convening the Earthquake Prediction

Council. The USGS will see if the Council can act in a manner which protects the sensitivity of the information it considers and conclusions it reaches. USGS will also determine if adequate seismic detection capability exists in the U.S. and in Peru to monitor events predicted by Brady.[9]

In a November 21, 1980, phone conversation with OFDA, Filson said that USGS intended to "inform the Peruvian Government through the U.S. Embassy, Lima that the Earthquake Prediction Council was available and would evaluate the Brady prediction if requested by the GOP."[10] In fact, Filson received a memo dated that same day from his deputy for research in Reston, Roger Stewart. Stewart showed a good grasp of the scientific problems inherent in the prediction as well as a good grasp of some of the bureaucratic politics. His opening summary paragraph is blunt:

> The prediction of an earthquake in Peru by Brady and Spence should be dealt with by the Earthquake Prediction Evaluation Council whether the Peruvian Government requests it or not. These are several reasons for doing this: (1) The question of the reliability and scientific soundness of the prediction method is not going to be resolved until it is dealt with, and it's better to do it in the present case than to wait for a prediction in the U.S.; (2) Giesecke may not want to take the chance of requesting a possibly bad review if he is making hay in the present circumstances; (3) A dry run for the Council isn't a bad idea. I recommend convening the Council for its annual meeting and giving it this to chew on.[11]

Stewart argued for an "order" to Brady and Spence to prepare full, original, written explanations of Peruvian seismicity patterns (Spence) and the theory (Brady) to be submitted to the Council beforehand. He was especially emphatic about having Brady "set forth the theory in writing. This should be done in detail, with no omissions or references to other papers. It should be complete in itself."[12]

In Lima

Before Washington could respond to Lima 10336 officially, however, Alberto Giesecke took up the issue of a NEPEC evaluation. On November 25, 1980, he sent a formal letter to U.S. Ambassador Edwin Corr, who reviewed it and sent the text in a cable, "Lima 10984," to the State Department on December 2. The key paragraph in Giesecke's letter was as follows: "In the name of the official entity in charge of seismological studies in Peru, I should like to request from you a formal statement from the National Earthquake Prediction Evaluation Council . . . with respect to the scientific validity of Dr. Brian T. Brady's prediction about the occurrence of a devastating earthquake which is to affect Lima and all the Southern Coast in August 1981, as well as the credibility level which can be given to such prediction."[13]

Giesecke also noted that the sudden worldwide media attention given the prediction after Clarence Allen's disclosure worried the Peruvians. They saw the possibility of a significant negative economic impact:

> The publication of articles such as those appearing in the *Miami Herald* on November 10 and in other newspapers in your country (another one was published in the *New York Times*) and in Europe, unfortunately do have a negative economic impact for Peru which

can be significant unless clarifying statements are made. It is possible to conceive that those planning to invest in Peru would be tempted to wait until after the predicted disaster does not take place; tourists likewise will not be anxious to visit a dangerous country; insurance premiums will go up; the Peruvian export market could suffer decreased prices, etc. While it is impossible to say for sure that this will happen or to estimate the impact, it is certainly a possibility.[14]

Giesecke closed his letter to Ambassador Corr with a request for a status report on the proposal to upgrade IGP. Lima 10984 itself closed with the Embassy position that the Giesecke request for the NEPEC evaluation "coupled with President Belaunde's . . . continuing interest" constituted the necessary diplomatic formalities to convene NEPEC.

Although the State Department "excisers" had a cutting spree with it, we obtained a different and even more interesting Confidential cable to Washington from U.S. Ambassador Corr. This November 28, 1980, cable, "Lima 10889," was entitled "President Belaunde Requests Authoritative Analysis of Brady's Earthquake Prediction Theory and Aid to Monitor Seismic Activity." Unfortunately, even after appealing the "national security" deletions, we have virtually nothing on President Belaúnde's request. Left to us, however, is a good picture of escalating reaction in Lima to the Brady-Spence prediction and obvious Embassy vexation with delays and bureaucratic politics in Washington. Lima 10889 acknowledged that the Brady-Spence prediction should be viewed with skepticism, but it noted the following:

While the Brady model is in doubt, there is a local psychological disaster model which is proceeding right on schedule. News media are filled with reports of earthquakes and seismic activity. Outbound airline flights in later July and early August of 1981 are already solidly booked. Cocktail party conversations frequently turn to Brady. U.S. mission employees are discreetly planning home leave, transfers and R&Rs to get themselves out of Lima during the July–August period of 1981. These psychological foreshocks are in the 2 to 3 range, but we can expect them to mount in the coming months.[15]

After several (deleted) paragraphs, Lima 10889 turned to Washington (implicitly USGS) footdragging on a concrete response to Lima 10336 and argued that time was of the essence:

> We understand there is reluctance in certain Washington bureaucracies to provide equipment that might seem to be in response to Brady's prediction and thereby lend greater credence to it. However, the Brady prediction exists and must be dealt with here in Peru. We strongly reiterate our recommendation that the assistance requested in Lima 10336 be provided so that the Peruvian Geophysical Institute can more accurately and extensively monitor seismic data, without the psychologically disturbing 3 or 4 month delay in processing data which is now the case.
>
> We appreciate that a revolutionary departure such as Brady's must cause disturbance in the scientific community, but we do not want professional jealousies and turf battles to keep us from dealing adequately with a growing psychological problem here. Brady is front page news in Peru and attention is focused on next summer. The concern is getting to the point that Peruvians fear it can adversely affect in-

vestment and development. To help deal with that psychological problem, we would like an authoritative USG assessment of the Brady prediction, but right now we need the assistance requested in Reftel B [Lima 10336].[16]

The Washington Response to Lima 10336

The official Washington response to the U.S. Embassy in Lima was a Limited Official Use cable, "State 324986," of December 8, 1980. This five-page cable is critically important because it embodies what would be official U.S. government policy on the Brady-Spence prediction. First, the cable reiterated that "highly qualified and respected USGS and NASA geophysicists" did not take Brady's theory or the prediction seriously. Second, State 324986 reported that USGS supported the idea of upgrading IGP capabilities but that this had to be "decoupled" from the prediction. Moreover, in order to further disguise this assistance, a "regional approach" was desirable. The cable was quite explicit:

A series of interagency meetings have been held to formulate preliminary USG response to Andean earthquake hazard and Brady prediction for Peru. GOP authorities again should be informed that the USG does not endorse the Brady prediction and that Drs. Brady and Spence speak only on their own behalf. However, because there is a high earthquake hazard in the Andean Region generally and for Peru particularly, we want to cooperate in all practical ways to ensure that the countries of the region accurately understand the nature and potential effects of this seismic risk and that they take all prudent measures to protect their populations. Consideration of any USG program of assistance in this regard is predicated on concern that the accepted general threat posed by seismic anomalies should be divorced from any specific prediction.[17]

The cable also confirmed that a NEPEC review of the Brady-Spence prediction would be set for late January 1981. Interestingly, it also reported that Spence required "teleseismically locatable earthquakes . . . in the Brady target zone" by January, or he would withdraw his support for the prediction. The final sections of the cable dealt with technical and procedural questions about methods to upgrade the IGP seismic detection network.

As Lima 10336 was a classic action request, the responding State 324986 was a classic bureaucratic compromise. Every principal saw something in his interest, but no one could be completely happy. Brian Brady would finally have the audience he had always wanted. The atmosphere would be charged, however, not neutral. John Filson, Rob Wesson, and their colleagues at USGS–Reston saw in State 324986 the official position that "the USG does not endorse the Brady prediction." At the same time, OFDA received a mandate to proceed with increased planning to respond to a disastrous earthquake, not only in Peru, but also in the Andean region generally. Giesecke and IGP in Lima did not see a clear confirmation of the prediction, but they did receive assurances that NEPEC would meet. They also received a major boost in their request for U.S. aid to upgrade their entire earthquake detection system. For USBM, one of their precocious young scientists was about to step fully into the media limelight.

On December 11, 1980, John Filson at USGS–Reston implemented the general agreement to convene NEPEC by writing all of the council members. He asked them to convene in Golden, Colorado, on January 26–27, 1981, to hear Brian Brady and William Spence.

Review

It is becoming glaringly obvious that two of the most important factors influencing the evolution of this scientific controversy were "extrascientific": (1) an action agency (OFDA) which saw the issues less in terms of scientific questions than in terms of organizational responsibilities and opportunities, and (2) media coverage of the prediction, which initially changed the stakes of the controversy when it began in Lima in late 1979 and dramatically affected both the number and the attitudes of the individuals involved as well as the organizational/reputational stakes of the game when it started in the U.S. in late 1980.

To fully appreciate OFDA's perspective, we should recognize that it regularly has to function abroad in two very different and difficult political situations. In its reactive mode, OFDA is the lead U.S. agency in time of disaster, when relief and recovery are usually the top policy priorities of a stricken nation. In normal times, however, OFDA is in the proactive stance of trying to promote hazard mitigation and enhance disaster preparedness, policies which are usually so far down the priority list for most governments as to be practically invisible. Therefore, a prediction such as the Brady-Spence prediction would be seen by OFDA as a way out of a very frustrating situation, for it suddenly raised the political salience of preparedness in Peru and offered the possibility of greatly increasing the efficiency of the U.S. emergency response if the earthquake did occur. Small wonder that

OFDA and USGS leadership saw the same situation very differently.

We should also note that several key participants in the Brady-Spence affair have argued that OFDA's lead role can be attributed to the indefatigable Paul Krumpe. That is, Krumpe is blamed for keeping the controversy alive when it would otherwise have faded away. The accusation does not hold, however. It is true that Krumpe was often highly visible to those outside OFDA, but the documentary record indicates significant support from superiors such as Dalton, Van Egmond, and Mitchell. In sum, Krumpe may have been the most outspoken Brady advocate, but his activities reflected *organizational* motivations at least as much as personal conviction.

The question of the proper role of the media in scientific controversies remains troubling. A lead editorial in a 1978 issue of *Science* put the general problem of contemporary science quite succinctly:

> In the past, professional tradition has largely prevented or corrected bad science. Peer review and editorial discretion have promoted the scientific quality of published works; the responsibility and joy of scientists in confirming or denying published conclusions have led to the eventual obscurity of bad science.
>
> But these professional procedures are being bypassed because of the needs of the times. The traditional outlet for scientific reporting is often short-circuited. Scientific work appears in unrefereed reports, news statements, hearing records, symposium transcripts, speeches, and independently published documents.[18]

In the case of the Brady-Spence prediction, the media saw news value in the controversy and became a kind of "science court" itself. Then, as we shall shortly see, the media put the real science court, NEPEC, under a microscope. Obviously, there is no easy solution to the problem encountered by traditionally slow-paced, self-correcting science when it falls into the electronically swift public environment of today.

SIX

Brady's 1981 "Trial":
The First Day

Background

Although USGS had had an in-house earthquake prediction evaluation group since the mid-1970s, a general feeling existed within USGS that a more formal system should be created, preferably with enough outside experts to counter the image of a "USGS club." In 1975, the state of California had established the California Earthquake Prediction Evaluation Council (CEPEC), and federal officials saw this as a model for an analogous organ at the national level.

According to its 1979 charter, the National Earthquake Prediction Evaluation Council (NEPEC) advises the director of USGS on the "completeness and scientific validity" of an earthquake prediction "made by other scientists, from within or outside of Government." That is, NEPEC was to specifically *avoid* "predictions based on data gathered by the Council itself."[1] The director of USGS makes the ultimate decision on whether or not to issue a formal earthquake prediction.

The NEPEC charter establishes that there will be between eight and twelve member scientists, all appointed by the director of USGS for staggered three-year terms. The charter stipulates that at least one-half of the members, as well as the chairman, "shall be other than USGS employees." The chief of the USGS Office of Earthquake Studies is stipulated vice-chairman. In January 1981, NEPEC had the following members: Dr. Clarence Allen, California Institute of Technology, chairman; Dr. John Filson, USGS–Reston, vice-chairman; Dr. Keiiti Aki, Massachusetts Institute of Technology; Dr. T. Neil Davis, University of Alaska; Dr. E. R. Engdahl, USGS–Denver; Mr. Neil C. Frank, National Hurricane Center; Dr. David P. Hill, USGS–Menlo Park; Dr. Thomas V. McEvilly, University of California, Berkeley; Dr. C. B. Raleigh, USGS–Menlo Park; Dr. James C. Savage, USGS–Menlo Park; Dr. Jerry C. Stephens, USGS–Reston; Dr. Lynn R. Sykes, Columbia University; Dr. Robert E. Wallace, USGS–Menlo Park.

In various international presentations, NEPEC Chairman Clarence Allen described the Council as having a "quasi judicial" function, in line with the charter responsibility "to provide objective and critical review by a uniform process, of any scientific data or interpretation of scientific data that might warrant issuance of a formal USGS prediction."[2]

In preparation for the January 26–27 meeting, Vice-Chairman John Filson sent a packet of background materials to the NEPEC members. This packet included Brady's "Theory of Earthquakes" (I–IV) and the NEIS Peruvian seismicity reports for September and October. It did not, however, include Brady's subsequent article "Anomalous Seismicity prior to Rock Bursts."[3] In a formal January 13, 1981, memo to the director of the Bureau of Mines, Rob Wesson (for USGS Director Menard) also requested "that any written materials to be used by Dr. Brady in his presentation be distributed to the Council beforehand so that they may be studied in depth."[4] It should be noted that NEPEC received no such supplementary materials.

The leadership of both USGS and USBM were worried about their conflicts over the Brady-Spence prediction surfacing in front of the media during the NEPEC meetings. John Filson at USGS–Reston called Chi-shing Wang at USBM–Washington at least three times between January 12 and January 16. According to Wang's handwritten notes, entitled "Brady's Trial," he and Filson agreed that open conflict between two agencies of the Department of the Interior should be avoided, that "a coordinated position of Interior Department should be developed in advance of the meeting."[5] A primary concern was reporter requests for interviews with the principals. Filson was afraid that the interviews posed the danger of "preempting the official statement of USGS Director," because "the [NEPEC] official recommendation will take 1–2 weeks to reach USGS Director."[6]

As a result of the Filson-Wang conversations, USBM–Washington determined that Donald Rogich (USBM–Washington) and Wang would attend the NEPEC meeting and that senior officials of the USBM Denver Research Center might also attend. All USBM officials were warned, however, that they were "to be cautious about making any comments which may appear to preempt the official position of the Department of Interior that shall be determined on the basis of [NEPEC recommendations]."[7]

During the month prior to the NEPEC meeting, Paul Krumpe—in his capacity as OFDA science advisor—also prepared to attend the Golden meeting. On December 21, 1980, Krumpe wrote to Van Egmond, requesting permission to attend the NEPEC meeting. Krumpe argued that his presence "as an observer . . . is extremely important to ensure that OFDA obtains objective detailed scientific analysis of the proceedings and conclusions derived therefrom." Krumpe again put the burden of proof on NEPEC:

> The Prediction Council meeting . . . represents possibly the last real opportunity to understand Brady's predictive assumptions, physical hypothesis and methodology of prediction. . . . If Brady's assumptions are invalid then the prediction will be negated; *however, if the scientists assembled cannot invalidate Brady's assumptions,* then the outcome of the meeting will take on new dimensions and perhaps lead to further cooperation, assistance and sharing of information and data between Brady, IGP, and possible emergent proponents of further analysis and data collection.[8]

NEPEC was to convene January 26, but a January 23, 1981, memo casts a great deal of initial, and still some lingering, doubt on the propriety of the whole NEPEC process. The memo was from USAID–Washington official Ronald Nicholson to Alan Van Egmond at OFDA. The very public nature of the NEPEC meetings, the presence of the world media, and the international implications of the findings were all of interest to Nicholson and had brought him into the controversy: "Per our discussions and after consultation with C. Paolillo [USAID–Latin America] I called ARA [Bureau for Inter-American Affairs] Acting Assistant Secretary [of State] John Bushnell to register our concern over the way the NEPEC will be convened. He expressed his general support of my suggestions and asked that I speak to DAS [Deputy Assistant Secretary of State] Samuel Eaton which I did."[9]

That is, the Brady case and the NEPEC evaluation meeting had reached the "attention level" of an assistant secretary (Bushnell) and deputy assistant secretary (Eaton) of state. Then came the bombshell of the Nicholson memo:

Eaton, anticipating my call, had spoken to the State Desk John A. Purnell. He informed me that Purnell said he had spoken to USGS and been assured that they would give us a definitive decision from the Council on Monday or Tuesday and that the decision would be negative. Purnell responded that USGS already had a "commission" working on Brady's theory and were convinced that their work would result in a quick Council decision completely "debunking" the Brady model.

I remarked that I was surprised by the apparent "star chamber" proceedings given seriousness of Brady's prediction and publicity (rightfully or wrongfully) it has received. I also suggested that USGS would be hard pressed to deny theory categorically given the inadequacy of the data base—reasoning that USGS reports on technical and equipment inadequacies of the IGP implied their acceptance of thesis that Peru now does not have an adequate info base to allow us to either discard or embrace Dr. Brady's mechanistic prediction model.[10]

It turns out that Purnell had indeed been in contact with Filson at USGS in Reston, because Purnell had to plan for the different diplomatic contingencies which could result from NEPEC's findings. In the course of their numerous pre-NEPEC conversations, Purnell asked Filson what he thought would happen. Filson responded by saying that (1) USGS people had been looking at Brady's prediction "for years" and thought little of his theory, and (2) he had known all the NEPEC members for many years and could hardly believe that they would find for Brady.[11]

Purnell then relayed the substance of these conversations to his superior Eaton, probably saying it a bit more forcefully (hence the references to a USGS "commission" and a "debunking"). As Nicholson picked this up from Eaton and passed it along to Van Egmond (and thence to Krumpe), the subsequent perception of conspiracy grew. The perception was probably inaccurate, however. The USGS–Reston files on NEPEC show draft press releases of *three* possible outcomes of the NEPEC meeting: (1) a positive evaluation, (2) a negative evaluation, and (3) too little information to decide. Viewed in conjunction with the interview material, these draft press releases indicate that Filson passed to Purnell a *personal* estimate of the likely NEPEC outcome, not an assured prejudgment.

Nicholson closed his memo to Van Egmond with another intriguing statement, this time focusing on the public nature of the NEPEC meeting:

Turning to the question of public nature of Council's deliberation (openness to media and press) [I] expressed our concern that anything less than a complete turndown of the Brady prediction (e.g., a recommendation to seek further data) would almost certainly set off a new round of speculation and panic in Peru and because of possible effects in South Pacific and Hawaii, in the U.S. press as well. Eaton asked if it were too late to "close" Council proceedings. I replied that I didn't know but suggested he call USGS Director Menard to express our concern on both points.[12]

U.S. Embassy–Lima's concern over the effects in Peru of the NEPEC evaluation is well illustrated by an unclassified January 27 warning cable:

Sensational first page headlines carried in most Lima dailies January 26 raised public consciousness once more on the Brady earthquake prediction. Triggering the extensive and alarmist (e.g., "Brady announces 9.9 earthquake for September") coverage is the convoking of the Earthquake Prediction Council in Golden, Colorado to consider Brady's forecast. AP, EFE and AFP wire service reports serve as the basis for most of the prominently placed stories which have been further embellished by imaginative local headline writers. . . .

The heightened awareness of the Peruvian populace to the earthquake prediction means that press coverage of the conclusions of the Golden meeting will be extremely crucial in determining the degree of public panic. The initial reporting has done anything but allay fears. As a result, we recommend that great care be exercised by the participants in the Golden meeting when speaking to the press.[13]

The Meeting Opens

When NEPEC convened at 8:30 A.M. on January 26, 1981, at the Colorado School of Mines in Golden, Colorado, only eight voting members were present. Interestingly, five of the eight were USGS employees. The voting attendees were Clarence Allen (Cal Tech), John Filson (USGS–Reston), James Savage (USGS–Menlo Park), E. R. Engdahl (USGS–Golden), David Hill (USGS–Menlo Park), C. B. Raleigh (USGS–Menlo Park), Thomas McEvilly (UC–Berkeley), and Lynn Sykes (Columbia). Dr. James Rice of Brown University, a specialist in rock physics, also attended the NEPEC meeting as a nonvoting expert consultant. The other NEPEC members were unable to attend because of prior commitments.

While inconsistent with the spirit of the NEPEC charter, which specified that at least one-half of the members "shall be other than USGS employees," USGS dominance at the Brady evaluation was allowed by the NEPEC quorum rule: "Four voting members will represent a quorum provided at least two non-USGS employees are present."[14] In this case, there were actually three non-USGS employees present (Allen, McEvilly, and Sykes), so the quorum rule allowed *any number* to complete the group, giving the five USGS employees who could attend a numerically dominant position.

Skirmishing

Vividly illustrating the very public nature of the NEPEC hearing (approximately two hundred people were present), the initial minutes of the first day were spent setting up the floodlights and cameras of the TV crews and laying out ground rules for the media. The first substantive order of business was the agenda, and the discussion immediately reflected a clear lack of planning, or at least a clear lack of communication between NEPEC and Brady. Chairman Clarence Allen opened with a "suggestion" that Brady and Spence have a total of five hours the first day to "get out everything that they think is important." Noting that he had counted on a two-day meeting, Brady responded that five hours might suffice for the background but not for the prediction itself. Allen replied that the Council would need time to deliberate and that "certainly we hope this thing doesn't drag on into next week."[15]

Several weeks earlier, Spence had suggested to Filson that he and Brady needed a day and a half to present, and now he tried to resurrect his original idea. He failed:

> DR. SPENCE: We can guarantee our presentation will be finished by noon tomorrow.
>
> CHAIRMAN ALLEN: We will ask you to make the presentation complete by this afternoon. Under what de-

gree you will continue tomorrow will be our decision, but what we are asking you to do is condense things to the point where we do get as much out of it as possible within the five hour presentation plus the give and take of the panel today.[16]

Ultimately, Brady acceded to the five-hour total, but the hearing had started badly, especially with the media observing. Of course, the fundamental problem was that the Council had very little written material to go on, only Brady's old articles and a few memoranda. Brady replied that he had originally planned for a March NEPEC meeting (after Allen's return from a trip to China) but that, anyway, "what I will be talking about is very much new." Council member Sykes noted that in the future NEPEC should have a simple statement of the prediction and a written description of the supporting data beforehand.[17] Sykes was to express repeatedly his displeasure at the lack of "clear documentation" in this case.

Brady opened his formal presentation by describing how his early (1974–75) discussions with Spence had convinced him that the unusually short aftershock sequence to the October 1974 earthquake near Lima indicated (to him) that "the process that will culminate in a large earthquake had indeed developed at that time." He noted that his 1976 statements in *Pure and Applied Geophysics* were really a "forecast" and that it was his subsequent theoretical and experimental work on rock failure which gave him a theory, a model, on which to base a prediction. As Brady explained: "What you need in order to develop a specific prediction is development of a clock, and that is what I believe I have done in the past several years. And this is what I want to get across to you, that [there] is indeed a clock, and that this clock is seismistic-patterned, and it is a space-time pattern."[18]

With Allen's permission, Brady spoke for approximately one hour, spending most of that time explaining his laboratory experiments on rock failure. Using visual aids, Brady tried to explain how he saw the relationship between stress, energy density, vibration, tensor potential, and so forth. He explicitly noted that he was using an approach "very similar to what we would call Einstein's [Field] Equation."[19]

Problem: Lack of a Common Framework

Shortly thereafter, however, a small revolt broke out, and the interchange clearly revealed the NEPEC quandary: How could they evaluate something which they admittedly did not understand and for which they were unprepared?

> CHAIRMAN ALLEN: There has been a request from members of the committee that we stop this, because no one really is understanding what is going on. I guess my comment is, that we have a prediction made by these two gentlemen that has a million people on the verge of panic right now, and I think we have been asked by the Peruvian Government to evaluate this. . . .

> DR. SAVAGE: May I reply to that, that we were given some preliminary information on this. It didn't contain anything like this. We didn't bone up on relativity. We didn't bone up on Maxwell's equation either. . . .

A minute later:

> CHAIRMAN ALLEN (TO BRADY): I hope you appreciate that you are turning members of the Council off to some degree by partly coming up with informa-

tion that we have not been advised about, despite the fact that it has been known for months that this meeting was going to take place, and the prediction itself has been over a year ago.

[incidental material omitted]

At the end of five hours, if you have not really come to the Peruvian prediction, in our opinion that is simply what we will say, and I just warn you ahead of time that we have allotted you five hours, and at the end of five hours, you say by the way we need another five hours, I think you can expect our reaction to be very negative.

DR. SAVAGE: This isn't a criticism, but I say, I don't think members of the panel have understood what you are saying. You are wasting your time, and you had better get to something that is perhaps within our comprehension, or present it more thoroughly so we can understand it.[20]

Brady attempted to respond by saying that he knew that his approach was "different" but that it was "good physics . . . not magic."[21] The problem was that the Council felt itself unprepared, and Council member Savage laid the blame at Brady's door:

DR. SAVAGE: If you were in the state you were four years ago and had someone present this to you in fifteen minutes, would you have comprehended it and been able to criticize it intelligently?

DR. BRADY: No.

DR. SAVAGE: That is the state we are in, and you are trying to present it to us, and just an iota of intelligence would have suggested that you send some of this out to us a month in advance so we could have become familiar with it, and I think you had at least a month's notice of this.[22]

Allen ruled that Brady should continue. Brady explained more about his laboratory work on rock failure and then moved on to a description of (successful) rock burst predictions in mines which had saved lives. After a brief recess, Brady suggested that questions might be in order. Chairman Allen concurred.

The questions focused exclusively on the rock burst prediction experiences of the Bureau of Mines in general and of Brady in particular. The critical questions revolved around the linkage between the rock burst predictions and Brady's theory. The Council members appeared to doubt that they were connected. Chairman Allen asked: "The way you drew those boxes to indicate the clustering left me a little bit concerned if somebody else would have drawn the boxes in the same places. . . . Is there really some statistical justification for the clustering as you claim it to be?"[23] Brady replied, but he was to cause himself more problems: "The clustering occurs in both space and time. We will see a burst of activity, and then as you quiet down, another burst, and then you could see one or two events, something like that, usually a couple of events, and it will quiet down again. Now, using all the data collected, because oftentimes earthquakes have so much, where do you stop it, how do you know where the aftershock zone is going to be? Fortunately in a mine, after all the activity was concentrated in that one area, you didn't have anything outside, so I used all the data, bar none."[24]

After other questions by Filson, Raleigh, and Allen, Rob Wesson, "representing the USGS Office of the Director," broke in:

> Dr. Wesson: So basically, he made the successful prediction of the mine burst as soon as he began to see a large, relatively a large, amount of small earthquakes within the mine?

CHAIRMAN ALLEN: That was the alarm?

DR. BRADY: Yes.

DR. WESSON: It didn't have anything to do with the quiet period and the active period, it was simply the main burst of the precursor seismicity?

DR. BRADY: Yes. Of course, the standard rule was—

DR. WESSON: In fact, the successful prediction of the mine burst didn't have anything whatsoever to do with anybody's model, it was just empirical observations. We are having a lot of little earthquakes, occasionally these have occurred prior to the big burst, let's get the people out.[25]

Upon reflection, the presence and active role of Wesson in the NEPEC deliberations raise questions. First, how could he participate? The NEPEC charter does not include any role *in the deliberations* for the Office of the USGS Director. Nor was Wesson listed as a NEPEC member at that time. Second, if Wesson was allowed to participate as a kind of "friend of the court," then why was Brady not allowed the same privilege? The participation of Wesson would prove especially critical on the second day.

The 1971 "Retrodiction"

At any rate, after a lunch break, Chairman Allen opened the afternoon session by again giving Brady the floor, and Brady turned to his "retrodiction" of the 1971 San Fernando, California, earthquake. He stated that he had obtained the seismicity records for the San Fernando area from 1932 on and, using his model, found that they conformed to his theory and that the earthquake had been "predictable": "What I would have done, and I truly mean this, given this data here, I would have predicted that earthquake. There is not any doubt in my mind that I would have said they are going to have an earthquake, and that its occurrence time would be within roughly 3,202 days from the end of this phase, and that is what I would have done at the time. There is no doubt in my mind."[26]

By bringing up one of the most intensively studied earthquakes in history, Brady had stepped fully onto many of the Council members' turf. They may have been "confused" about Brady's unified theory, his interpretation of laboratory results, and the Bureau of Mines rock burst predictions, but on the 1971 San Fernando earthquake, they were confident and direct. Chairman Allen was especially incredulous that Brady could have given him a prediction. McEvilly, Engdahl, Filson, Savage, Sykes, Raleigh, and Wesson then all aggressively questioned Brady on (1) his lack of precise knowledge about the 1971 damage patterns, but most importantly (2) the very vague criteria which he putatively would have used to delineate the shapes and locations of the various "zones" necessary for his theory. The Council was clearly unconvinced that Brady had criteria and decision rules specific enough to separate pre-earthquake "wheat from chaff," noting that hindsight made theoretical *retro*dictions much easier than real-life *pre*dictions.[27]

William Spence

After Brady's presentation on San Fernando, Chairman Allen called on William Spence to make his presentation. Spence proved much easier to understand, largely because he restricted himself to familiar plate tectonic arguments. He began with a tectonic history of the boundary between the Nazca Plate and the South American Plate, noting that some of the world's greatest earthquakes and tsunamis were generated in the Peru-Chile Trench. Using a relative plate motion figure of ten centimeters a year and reducing the total for observed slip, Spence argued that a full twenty meters of slip were unaccounted for.

Spence pointed to strain data to support his position as well as to data on the uplift of the entire coastline north and south of Lima. Spence illustrated with a slide of what is probably the fastest and largest uplift in the world at the present time: "I took this slide when I was in the City of Pisco in October of 1980. I am standing on the sea wall that joins to this wharf that goes out into the Pacific Ocean that was built in 1940. As you can see, about half of this wharf is now on the beach. I talked to people that said this was a swimming hole when they were boys . . . and now it is high and dry."[28]

Spence adduced more data from plate studies around the world to underscore his position that the Nazca and South American Plates had not "decoupled." His major point was that "if plates decoupled, ordinarily there are normal faulting earthquakes near the oceanic trench. . . . There have been no normal faulting earthquakes since we had data on central Peru and Northern Chile."[29]

Spence then argued that the earthquakes predicted by Brady were "tectonically plausible." He stuck by his colleague: "I would say that we have predictions of really major earthquakes in Central Peru and Northern Chile. We have a tectonic situation that is such, that perhaps an earthquake of this size is a possibility. So we have some conditional probability that this event will occur."[30]

After an hour, Chairman Allen opened up the session for Council members' questions. Not surprisingly, they focused on the accuracy of the earthquake data (precise location and magnitude) for the Peru-Chile Trench and on other possible interpretations of that seismicity. Where the Council really pressed Spence was on the specific relationship between Spence's rather conventional tectonic arguments and Brady's radical deterministic model, and on Spence's assessment as a scientist of that model. Chairman Allen asked: "Similar to what you just stated, you sort of summarized your tectonic theory with a statement to a very large earthquake, that perhaps an earthquake of this size is a possibility, which is a rather carefully phrased, but not a very strong statement. You then went on to point out that the conditional probability would be increased if the normal fault earthquake would occur down dip. Do I infer as of the moment, that you think the probability of the big earthquake occurring is really very low?"[31] Spence gave a rather contradictory answer:

> My feeling on the probability of the predicted earthquake is that it may be *fairly low*. I think that we have a prediction model that is dependent. It has predicted foreshocks to occur, and they haven't occurred in exactly the same way as they were originally predicted to occur. I recognize there is not a person in this room who has ever predicted an earthquake. It is an incredibly difficult problem, so I think the predicter has the right to update a prediction. However, the predicted foreshock activity which is supposed to originate between October and the end of December of this year, apparently recently on December 26th, this is preliminary, there was a foreshock of 4.5 magnitude that occurred essentially in the same place as the inclusion zone forming events of 1974, which I carefully pointed out when we went through the preseismicity of the 1974 earthquake, because this earth-

quake is teleseismic, and it last occurred, as a matter of fact, in the middle of the target zones. So it seems my personal assessment of the conditional probability of the main shock is now *increased*.[32]

More discussion of the meaning of observed seismicity in terms of the Brady model followed, but one particular comment stood out. Barry Raleigh evinced qualms about the "dynamic" nature of the prediction. That is, it was changing too often for his comfort: "You guys have made a model dependent deterministic prediction, so I am told, right, but you tell me you are going to keep changing that as time goes on, as it suits you, as your model changes, or as data influences you. . . . That is not the way or the kind of thing we can deal with, and certainly not the kind of thing the Peruvians can deal with."[33]

Spence continued without serious challenge and then, with Chairman Allen's permission, turned the presentation back over to Brady for another hour. Building on Spence's general arguments, Brady noted that it was the similarity between the pre-1971 San Fernando seismicity and the recent earthquake patterns in the Lima area which led to his prediction. Brady went on at great length to describe and explain what he saw as similar situations—but with the seismic potential much larger offshore Lima, of course.

Questions from the Floor

As the day drew to a close, Chairman Allen opened the session to questions and comments from the audience. The first to comment was Dr. Oscar Miró Quesada, representing "the [Peruvian] scientific community," but also a member of the most powerful media family in the country. After questioning Brady about his personal certitude of the prediction, Miró Quesada reminded everyone of the situation in Lima:

> You must understand, and everybody else, the situation down home. The scientific community has the responsibility of discussing the matter, but the layman, the general psychosis that is being produced by this prediction in my country is quite—well, something that really scares us, and that is one of the reasons our Government has asked the United States Government to have this meeting. If you have something more solid on what to stand on, and if that prediction comes true, like we all hope it won't, but if it comes true . . . What will happen is all of Lima would be wiped off the map.[34]

A few questions later, audience member James Deterich (USGS–Menlo Park) zeroed in on the fundamental paradigm challenge of the Brady model, the "scale invariant" argument:

> First of all, throughout these experiments, you have equated fractional intact rock with the earthquake process. I think the evidence [for] this is fairly scanty. . . .
> And also equating emissions and laboratory experiments with the earthquake events, and I think there is certainly room for a lot of opinion on this subject, but certainly my opinion is that acoustic emissions are at best a very rough analogue of earthquake processes. They generally are recognized as arising from tensile cracking of individual grains within the sample, and just how this relates to large scale shear ruptures requires something of an act of faith, and I really don't have that faith.[35]

Paradigm Issues

After a few more, rather desultory interchanges, Chairman Allen tried to terminate the day's meeting. This was not to be, however, for Rob Wesson raised a set of issues fundamental to the entire NEPEC deliberations. Various Council members then joined in. The day was not over.

Wesson started by saying that everyone in the room probably agreed that the plate tectonic picture indicated great earthquake potential along the South American coast, although quibbles on details could be expected. He was much more concerned, however, about "the actual arguments for time-space magnitudes," and whether other scientists would see and interpret similarly the seismicity "patterns" of Brady and Spence. Wesson then came to the crux of the issue: Was the Brady model within the tradition of "normal science," or was it a truly radical departure? As Wesson said:

> I guess we are in a little bit of a philosophical problem in that if we . . . had commonly shared an established knowledge in certain science and physics and mechanical processes and so on, we would be in good shape, and the Council should easily say this prediction is based on commonly accepted knowledge. In this case, we are requesting a bit beyond that, at least from what I understand from Brian. It would seem that the Council is going to have to judge . . . the model which Brian proposes: Is it a logical and reasonable extension of commonly understood and accepted knowledge and practice? If it is indeed logical, I suppose the Council can evaluate the prediction. If it is not, [and] the Council does not feel that Brian's model is a logical extension of commonly accepted understanding and knowledge, then

I think the Council [has] a very difficult problem. Then it does not seem possible to evaluate [the] prediction in a scientific setting, but requires some other reference frames.[36]

Barry Raleigh then pointed out that it was not yet clear how the specific prediction was "critically based [in] any important way on the theoretical model." According to Raleigh, all Brady and Spence had was a seismicity pattern of their "own particular determination," which they then interpreted. Brady responded by saying that the prediction was "very model dependent." Raleigh replied, "Tomorrow we need to know that."[37]

James Rice then asked for copies of Brady's slides and transparencies to study overnight. Thomas McEvilly asked for a "clear exposé" of the seismicity pattern and its interpretation. He was frustrated:

I am asking for the basis for your statements on Peru. You clearly set out [a] sequence of events that went to a prediction for August 31st of 1981, that we have seen piecemeal, and also the geometric relationship of those events that were selected to go into that group . . . sequence. I don't care about the San Fernando event. I don't care about the rock burst. I mean, they clearly bear on the problem. The thing that leaves me terribly frustrated is not being able to point a finger at a specific data on the map and say, where is this. We have to have that. I can't deal with the problem without it really. At least a summary of some sort that we can look at.[38]

Robert Engdahl criticized the quality of the earthquake data, noting uncertainties in epicenter location and incompleteness. He had "a lot of disturbing questions."[39]

McEvilly and Raleigh returned to their theme, the lack

101

of specific, logical connections between data, theory, and prediction:

> DR. MCEVILLY: I am having a bit of difficulty, I must admit, absorbing just the basic fundamentals of the sequence that has been constructed to extrapolate to. I think it is incumbent upon you to let us see which event. I don't know how far back you have to go, but there aren't more than a hundred events that we are talking about. Let's see these 100 events.
>
> DR. RALEIGH: You see, this is virtually incomprehensible. This sequence back and forth that we listened to this afternoon is almost impossible to follow, and there must be a better way to pull it together so that we can comprehend. If we can't comprehend it—[40]

Chairman Allen closed the session with the charge to Brady for the following day to show clearly and simply how everything tied together to yield the prediction for 1981. For Allen and the Council in general, *the burden of proof was clearly on Brady*: "It is incumbent upon you to try to convince us that these [connections] are rational."[41]

SEVEN

Hardball: The Second Day
of the Trial

A Change of Tone

Compared with the relatively low-key first day of the NEPEC meetings, the second day was belligerent. Brady remembers it as probably the worst day of his life, as well he should, for he was vigorously attacked on a variety of fronts.

Chairman Allen opened the morning session by turning it over to Brady, who was supposed to show the relationship between his general theory and the specific Peruvian prediction and to provide "a clear understanding of the [supporting] data."[1] Chairman Allen noted that he wanted to limit the discussion to an hour but that Brady had "the floor for the moment." That moment lasted about thirty seconds.

Brady started by discussing the 1974 Peruvian earthquake sequence and the fault characteristics of the offshore zones. Rob Wesson and then Thomas McEvilly broke in at this point, stating that they were unconvinced that the appropriate fault plane had been chosen and

103

asked if the resulting nucleating zone was a "crucial element to [the] model."[2] Brady replied that indeed it was crucial and that if he was wrong about the relative plate motion, then his prediction was in trouble: "If that showed completely different properties, if it showed a normal underthrust type mode, and no uplift in that zone, I would say that they were—well, I would have to really understand it, you know. I would probably be quite concerned about the prediction. Yes, I would. I would say that. That would be my statement. I would have to reinterpret the whole concept of this prediction."[3]

This was really only a preliminary, however, for the battle of the day would rage over the existence, nonexistence, or logical properties of the key element connecting theory and data: "equations." For example, Wesson asked for an explanation of the color pattern on a Brady slide: "I would be very interested, if you could at some point write down the equation on the board that you used to map for what you interpreted to be the inclusion zone, which I understand to be the '74 earthquake sequence, to the possible rupture area of the big earthquake in the coming year."[4]

Brady answered with a relationship between a nucleation zone, an "Ace of H," and an "Ace of C cosmological horizon." Robert Engdahl and James Rice then asked for a simple illustrative equation ignoring all the complicating factors. At this point, any remaining "good fellowship among scientists" wore off, and the exchanges began to exhibit hostility, not to mention sarcasm:

> Dr. Engdahl: I wonder if you could just for the moment assume a spherical geometry, and if you need a single crystal of quartz or some isotropic medium, can you write down the equation in going from Ace of H to Ace of C in the simplest possible case?

DR. BRADY: Depends on the characteristics of the zone. The best thing to do is give you examples of this, I think.

DR. ENGDAHL: I really want to see an equation. I am not convinced that you are [not] getting this out of that Tibetan Book of the Dead. For example, let's see an equation seriously.

DR. BRADY: I guarantee you it is not coming out of the Tibetan Book of the Dead. It is good mathematics and good physics.

DR. ENGDAHL: Let's see an equation for the simplest cases.

DR. RICE: I don't understand your reluctance. If we ask you to write down the equation for an elastic compendium, or elastic dialectic, or what have you, you can set down the set of field equations and the extension of the equations, and what have you. Why is this such a hard request?[5]

Brady attempted to respond, but each response seemed to generate new questions about the terms and meaning of the equation. For example, Brady related his equation to inclusion zones leading to laboratory rock failure, and Rice opened up another front, namely, Brady's knowledge of rock fracture research itself: "I guess I am looking at the problem from the point of view that . . . fracture has been studied, and it has been a scientific subject for a large number of years. There are many problems, especially relating to tensile fracture, which are reasonably understood, and solved, and I am trying to make some contact with that literature and with that body of knowledge and the concepts that you are putting forth here."[6]

Brady answered that he was describing "a critical nucleation zone that develops prior to the occurrence of the catastrophic failure." Brady then said that the evidence for this zone "destroys itself" in the failure, the imploding.[7] Rice countered: "This imploding, this is the bit of mysticism thrown into this. I see no observational bases for these concepts."[8]

Over the next several minutes, Raleigh, McEvilly, and Rice all questioned Brady's foundation in rock mechanics. Rice was especially blunt: "It seems to me you are avoiding the difficult theoretical problem that is well phrased in terms of existing knowledge of fracture and mechanics of materials." Then later: "You seem to be running off in some direction which has no observational or physical support at all, so I simply can't understand the whole motivation for what you are doing. I don't see how you can get started on this path."[9]

Wesson then turned the focus back to the equation question, asking for an "equation for the simplest case and see if we can't follow through on how that equation might be solved."[10] Brady responded with a discussion of "event" sequence and immediately became embroiled in an exchange with Savage and Raleigh on whether or not the events were "tensile or shear cracks."[11] Ultimately, Raleigh again questioned Brady's background knowledge: "You describe a process where a tensile crack opens up, and then somehow shears, and you imply, and I may be wrong in inferring this, that these more or less happen simultaneously, and I am trying to say, that is not internally consistent with what we know about tensile fracturing in . . . the stress field in which it takes place."[12]

Brady replied that in his laboratory tests a nucleation zone developed which led to faulting and ultimate failure. Wesson countered that there was considerable research and "plenty of interpretations" of rock failure "which don't require the kind of model that you [Brady] have outlined."[13]

An obviously beleaguered Brady responded that the jury was still out on rock failure but that "maybe this is all wrong. Maybe this theory is not needed."[14] The following very important exchange then took place, and the focus was again on a "normal science" equation with which the Council could grapple:

> DR. WESSON: If it is all wrong, then four and one-half million people in Peru are being agitated unnecessarily.
>
> DR. BRADY: That could be a risk, yes.
>
> DR. WESSON: It is a risk.
>
> DR. BRADY: Yes, I do know that very well.
>
> DR. WESSON: I would like to see if an equation exists that describes this posture. I would like to see it written down.
>
> DR. BRADY: I wanted to give the theory section yesterday.
>
> DR. WESSON: Brian, I will sit here as long as it takes for you to write down the equation for the simplest possible case. If you can convince me . . . as members of the scientific community, who build things from falling apples, and *if we can agree this is a logical extension of current knowledge and current interpretation, then we can all agree that this prediction is reasonable. If you cannot write an equation that we can all agree is some logical extension, then we are unnecessarily and unfairly agitating the people in Peru.*

A moment later:

> DR. SAVAGE: Brian, I think I understand conceptually what you are describing. Now, I may disagree with that, based on my interpretation and other data I have seen, but what I don't understand is the actual physical argument, because I don't see any equation. *You have described a qualitative model which could have come from any number of sources. It could have come from some analysis of some equations,*

107

and could have come from a dream, for all I know, but until I see that equation, I can't evaluate and I can't determine whether I would agree reasonably that it might be derived from the physics that we all understand.[15]

Thomas McEvilly then shifted the point of attack to the temporal relationship between the development of Brady's theory and the development of the Peru prediction. Suddenly, McEvilly was concerned that the theoretical formulation had not led to the prediction:

DR. McEVILLY: When you formulated the Peruvian prediction, as we know it, [had] you written down your thoughts about the cosmological horizons at that time?

DR. BRADY: Yes, I had in a way. The basic thinking is there.

DR. McEVILLY: So this theory is critical to the Peruvian prediction? That is the point?

DR. BRADY: Yes, it is. It is critical to any prediction.

DR. McEVILLY: I don't care about any but the Peruvian. We should operate on the assumption that the formulation that you are going to lay out for us is critical to the baby blue and the brown and the red areas on the map that leads to these specific deterministic Peruvian predictions. It is critical in your mind and preceded it in your mind?

DR. BRADY: No, it did not precede the mapping of these things, and formation of the zones is indeed critical. If you can prove this wrong, then this theory is wrong.

DR. McEVILLY: No, wait, I do have a chronology problem. What is the horse and what is the cart? Have you formulated this theory to substantiate a prediction that you made based on primarily spatial and temporal relationships among earthquakes in the area or vice versa?

DR. BRADY: The model predicts certain space-time patterns of seismicity. Before the failure, certain things must happen before it occurs. That is an integral part of the whole theory.

DR. RALEIGH: You are not responding to the question.

DR. BRADY: What comes first? The two are intertwined.

DR. MCEVILLY: We have the results in our hand. We have your very specific prediction. I don't know, from what I have heard, whether or not that prediction depends critically upon the theoretical element.

DR. BRADY: There are two ways you can go out there.

DR. MCEVILLY: Yes, you can do the theory, [or] you can do the prediction and cook up the theory. . . .

DR. BRADY: Both. I work with the data and I work with the theory, all the time. It is a continuous interplay. I just don't go off wildeyed theorizing.

DR. MCEVILLY: Is it possible to answer the question of the cart and the horse? Is the theory critical to the prediction? In other words, is the prediction based upon a theoretical framework that you are going to outline for us? Was it based upon the results of this theoretical development? Yes or no?[16]

Brady replied that he hated to say it, but "no and yes." He explained that seeing space-time seismicity patterns in the laboratory, in mines, and in past earthquakes allowed "a prediction based on data analysis alone with no theory to back it up."[17] Wesson could not let that statement pass: "I think that is a very important point, because there are all sorts of people around the world that predict all sorts of things based on cycles or numerology or any kind of analysis of data. Now, if that is the argument, and unless there is some strong physical arguments that make that sensible, then I don't think it is a scientific prediction. It is a numerological prediction."[18]

The Equation Issue

After a protracted technical discussion between Brady, Rice, McEvilly, and Wesson about tensile stresses, inclusions, principal axes, elasticity, and other concepts, Brady suddenly laid out an equation. The focal point was "Tau zero," and it captured the attention of the Council for an extended time.

Brady explained that "Tau zero in the [abstract] is proportionate to the area of the [inclusion] zone and the surface area," that it was the mathematical device for separating seismic events and clusters.[19] Wesson then recalled Brady's discussion of the 1971 San Fernando earthquake and saw a logical flaw: "Now, if Tau zero is proportional to the area, and the San Fernando area is a few tenths of a kilometer, and the Peru area . . . is in the hundreds of kilometers, you have an order of magnitude greater area. . . . Why is the Tau zero smaller for Peru?"[20]

In not very elegant terminology, Brady responded that the size of Tau zero depended on other variables as well, including "temperature [?] and precursor loading."[21] Wesson then said that he guessed that was why he needed a full equation for Tau zero.

Following this, Brady, Raleigh, and Savage went through another long exchange on tensile versus shear fracturing in laboratory rock breakage experiments. Raleigh repeatedly tried to make the point that laboratory experiments and even mine rock bursts bore no resemblance to great earthquakes, that the quantitative difference in scale made earthquakes a qualitatively different phenomenon. Of course, the opposite tenet was the crux of Brady's entire "scale invariant" approach.

Conditions for a Retraction

With a break included, most of the rest of the morning session was spent in relatively innocuous discussions of seismic data reliability (Engdahl versus Spence) and interpretation (Wesson versus Spence). The only contentious points again came when Brady discussed his equations. A key concession emerged, however, when James Savage and Brady discussed the precursory earthquakes "necessary" for Brady's prediction to continue, because Brady specified *when he would rescind his prediction*:

> DR. BRADY: I would certainly call this thing off in the spring, if there are no more foreshocks.
>
> DR. SAVAGE: May?
>
> DR. BRADY: May. You bet. May is where I put a time event. If large events don't develop, we will call that off.
>
> [incidental material omitted]
>
> If there are no foreshocks, the reading of the data is incorrect. That is possibly one of the good things, the beautiful thing, if the model works. If it is correct, . . . it is possible to minimize false alarm rates, because you do make predictions of when certain data should come in, and certain things should happen. If they don't happen, the data base is not correct. That is it. That is the basis for this whole thing.[22]

Chairman Allen evinced concern that because Brady's prediction had changed several times over the years, he might change it again. Allen, Raleigh, McEvilly, Savage, and Wesson then attempted to pin Brady down still further:

> DR. SAVAGE: At this midway calendar, when are you willing to call it off? What has to occur before then?

> DR. WESSON: I would like to, if we could go through a kind of month by month analysis of what Brian expects will happen, and if there [are] branches or sufficient conditions.

[incidental material omitted]

> DR. BRADY: If the interpretation is correct, I will expect to see larger foreshocks develop. They would have to begin developing in this general zone, large foreshocks.

[incidental material omitted]

> DR. RALEIGH: How many foreshocks do you need?

> DR. BRADY: About four to five. Now, I also will expect that there be events happening along what would be the eventual aftershock zone, and it would have to start coming in.

[incidental material omitted]

> DR. WESSON: There should be more earthquakes than we have seen over the last couple of decades; is that right?

> DR. BRADY: I can't tell you how many. I don't know, but I would expect to see a pick up. I would expect to see a pick up in activity.

> DR. WESSON: More earthquakes than we have seen over the last couple of decades on the average?

> DR. ENGDAHL: There has to be a basis for comparison.

DR. BRADY: Yes, I would say, yes.

DR. RALEIGH: How many foreshocks in that central nucleation zone do you require before you say these foreshocks are random events?

DR. BRADY: I don't know how many.

DR. RALEIGH: Would one satisfy you?

DR. BRADY: No, I would expect to have a fair number. I am not going to have an earthquake sequence like this, if you don't have a fair number of foreshocks.

DR. WESSON: A fair number is more than ten?

DR. BRADY: It would have to become quite active.

DR. WESSON: More than ten?

DR. BRADY: More than five [incidental material omitted] between now and mid-May. If I don't see events in there, I say I was probably wrong.[23]

Closure

Chairman Allen terminated the public portion of the NEPEC hearings by asking the Council members and then Brady and Spence for any closing statements. Barry Raleigh led off by noting that the presentations by Spence were plausible but not convincing, primarily because of inadequate or unreliable data. To Brady, however, he was less kind:

Brian's work, I think we pretty well covered that this morning, and just to sum up my impression of it. I don't think there is any theoretical depth developed . . . which adequately describes clustering of earthquakes in time. At least you have not presented it to us, despite repeated requests. The cyclical behavior, you have not really given us any theoretical develop-

113

ment to explain what occurs. We are waiting to hear. I would like to see it, but for some reason, you won't give it. Your previous public work has got errors in it, which we have not discussed, but it doesn't give me great confidence and great reliability in the so called work you are presenting here today.

[incidental material omitted]

In my opinion, the seismicity patterns that you purport to show here are clearly ad hoc, and I see no relationship to the theory. . . . Consequently, I think I feel apologetic to our Peruvian colleagues and to the people of Peru.[24]

James Savage added that he was actually quite satisfied with Spence's presentation but "really had trouble with Brady's presentation, and this is a reputation he has, that people simply do not understand what he is saying." Savage concluded that the only thing he was happy about was Brady's "clear map of what he expects to happen before mid-May," which provided a date for the retraction of the prediction.[25]

John Filson and Clarence Allen both noted that the lack of written materials by Brady and Spence had greatly hindered their own cause and hampered the working of the Council. Both also indicated that they hoped that the Council would not face similar situations in the future.

Spence and then Brady made brief closing remarks reiterating their positions, and Clarence Allen terminated the session with the following curious statement:

I will say on behalf of the Panel, we admire your stamina and your spirit. It was a real rough session for you, and we appreciate your willingness to go through it. I hope you also realize we are not here by choice. All of us would rather be somewhere else,

114

and this is not really the kind of forum which would ideally settle a scientific issue, which we are asked to be critical of our colleagues. Nevertheless, I think it is clear that earthquake prediction is a very special field. We all have certain social responsibilities, and I think this is the kind of thing we simply must go through.[26]

Verdict

With the idea of coming up with a consensus statement by the end of the day, Chairman Allen and Vice-Chairman Filson took the Council into executive session. From all accounts, there was no disagreement within the Council about the substance of their findings. They more or less accepted Spence's tectonic arguments but utterly rejected Brady's deterministic model and therefore the specific prediction. The only disagreements came on how harshly to phrase their reaction to Brady. The official NEPEC statement read as follows:

At the request of the Government of Peru, the director of the U.S. Geological Survey has convened the National Earthquake Prediction Evaluation Council to review the prediction of a major earthquake in Peru. Specifically, the prediction by Drs. Brian Brady and William Spence states that a series of large earthquakes will begin at the end of June 1981, off the coast of Peru.

The sequence is predicted to contain a magnitude 7.5–8.0 event on or about June 28, 1981, a magnitude 9.2 event on or about August 10, 1981, and a magnitude 9.9 event on or about September 16, 1981. The predicted epicenters of these events are all near

Lima. We understand that if there is not a substantial increase in the number of earthquakes of magnitude 4.5 or greater in a specific area off the coast of Peru by mid-May 1981, Drs. Brady and Spence will withdraw the prediction.

The members of the council are unconvinced of the scientific validity of the Brady-Spence prediction. The council has been shown nothing in the observed seismicity data, or in the theory insofar as presented, that lends substance to the predicted times, locations, and magnitudes of the earthquakes.

The council regrets that an earthquake prediction based on such speculative and vague evidence has received widespread credence outside the scientific community. We recommend that the prediction not be given serious consideration by the government of Peru.

We cannot say with complete confidence that major earthquakes will not occur at the predicted times, but we judge the probability of this happening to be very low indeed. On the basis of the data and interpretation currently available, none of the members of the council would have serious reservations about being present personally in Lima at the times of the predicted earthquakes.

We are particularly distressed that although this prediction has been publicized in various forms for several years, nothing in the scientific literature or in other written form has been made available to this council on the detailed theoretical basis and methodology of the Peruvian prediction as currently formulated. In fact, the prediction specified in a memorandum by Dr. Brady on May 1, 1980, is quite different from that presented orally at this meeting.

116

Our rejection of the specific prediction by Drs. Brady and Spence should not be taken as minimizing the risk to lives and property from earthquakes in Peru. Since its founding, Lima has experienced many strong earthquakes, and others must be expected in the future both there and elsewhere along the coastal regions of Peru. Despite the continuing need to prepare for earthquakes in Peru, we do not recommend any special measures in response to the Brady-Spence prediction.[27]

All the major television networks, the wire services, and many U.S. dailies carried stories on what they variously called the NEPEC "invalidation," "negation," or "rejection" of the Brady-Spence prediction. Perhaps the best story, however, was by Richard Kerr in *Science*. Entitled "Prediction of Huge Peruvian Quakes Quashed," the story succinctly explained Brady's approach:

Watching rocks under compression fail in the lab, Brady concluded that, before complete failure, small pockets of highly fractured rock form that are under tension. After further growth, the pockets, or inclusions, coalesce, the new pocket collapses, and the whole rock fails. On the larger scale of an earthquake, the inclusion collapse is the main shock. The theory's key to prediction, he says, is that once the process begins in the lab or in the earth, a "clock" begins running whose speed is steady until the final collapse. Bursts of moderate foreshocks are the ticks of the clock.[28]

Kerr reported that not a single member of the Council accepted the "scale invariant" argument. He also related that the Council (1) could see "no obvious theoretical

117

basis for the prediction," (2) complained that the prediction kept changing, (3) doubted the empirical base, and (4) believed that Brady was asking them "to take too much on blind faith."[29]

The NEPEC statement was officially transmitted by the State Department to President Belaúnde. Because of prior commitments, Alberto Giesecke did not attend the NEPEC evaluation meetings. Daniel Huaco, a senior IGP seismologist, did. No one appeared to notice the absence of Giesecke at the time, but it had implications which we will follow up in the next chapter.

Review: NEPEC in Retrospect

When NEPEC was created, the hope was that it would be called upon to render judgments on conventional earthquake predictions emanating from the mainline seismological community, not paradigm-challenging predictions made by irreverent outsiders. That is, NEPEC heard as its first case the exact opposite of the kind of case it wanted to hear.

In the Brady-Spence affair, NEPEC served as a kind of deformed science court. NEPEC was a jury, but several of the members also took turns as prosecutors, especially on the second day. Without reference to or blessing from the NEPEC charter, Rob Wesson of the Office of the USGS Director was allowed to participate, and he was quite aggressive on the crucial second day. NEPEC even had its own specialist on rock mechanics (James Rice) present, a surprise to Brady.

Brady and Spence, but especially Brady, were alone. They served as their own defense, and they had no "consultants." The burden of proof was on them, and the deck was stacked.

What USGS in general and NEPEC in particular failed to recognize was that the Brady-Spence evaluation was seventy-five percent *political theater* and only twenty-five percent science. *How* the Council members "did in" Brady was much more important than the substance of their critiques. By giving the impression of intense prejudice against Brady almost from the outset, the Council undercut its own credibility. NEPEC may have been scientifically correct, but the manner in which they carried out their tasks only increased distrust of the motives of USGS and contributed to the continuation of the controversy.

EIGHT

The Controversy Continues

In Peru

In late January 1981, coincident with the NEPEC meeting in Golden, an international team of disaster specialists was visiting Lima. The focus was on (1) Peruvian needs in the event of a major disaster, and (2) international assistance possibilities. The impetus for their visit was (again) the Brady-Spence prediction: "Recent publicity of predictions of earthquakes in Peru raised international awareness and increased public tension in Peru. The Government of Peru requested assistance from UNDRO and the United States, and the Peruvian Red Cross issued an appeal for materials and equipment with which to respond to a disaster."[1]

In their final report, the team noted that although available funds were clearly insufficient to meet Peruvian government and Red Cross requests, some technical assistance was possible. Reiterated several times, however, was team concern about the equipment and resources of Peruvian Civil Defense. In effect, the worry was that the key link in disaster preparedness and response in Peru,

Civil Defense, was also the weakest link: "The administrative procedures established to respond to a major disaster do not seem to be realistic, in light of the absence of operational procedures describing the role of the ministries. It is impossible to determine who, from what ministry, would be making the primary decisions during a disaster. It is most likely that the Peruvian military, which has an organized nationwide system, would be called upon to respond to a major disaster and probably make all important decisions."[2] More specifically, the team noted the fundamental bureaucratic/political weakness of Peruvian Civil Defense: "The response capability to any type of a major disaster is reduced by the lack of essential equipment and the organization's inability to carry out their legal mandate. This situation is due, in part, to the evident low priority status of that organization within the Government's overall structure."[3]

Interestingly, as the team was present in Lima at the time of the NEPEC hearing, they offered this observation of the effect:

> The decision of the U.S. Earthquake Prediction Council undoubtedly reduced some of the Peruvian anxiety about an imminent specific earthquake in the vicinity of Lima, but initial response to the decision indicates that the majority of the people still believe that a destructive earthquake affecting Lima will occur in the not too distant future. The high frequency of damaging earthquakes in Central Peru virtually ensures that this will in fact be the case. Therefore, the time is ripe to act while the awareness and interest of the people, the Government of Peru and the international community are still high.[4]

121

In the U.S.

Questions about the NEPEC meeting were surfacing in the U.S. literally within hours of its closing, even within USGS. Robert Evans, then USGS assistant director for the central region (working out of Denver), attended the NEPEC meeting and recalls being "appalled at the lack of professional integrity" displayed by the Council and "concerned about the reputation of the Survey, especially in front of the media."[5] On January 29, 1981, Evans sent an electronic memo to the director of USGS in Reston entitled "The Trial and Execution of Dr. Brian T. Brady." Calling the NEPEC procedures a "court martial," Evans expanded on the metaphor and suggested that for Brady and Spence the

> best defense would have been to throw themselves on the gentle mercy of the court and perhaps they could have received only a flogging. Nevertheless, they manfully and gentlemanly tried to present their case. After about 3 hours of testimony, the judges grew weary and protested loudly that it was too much, and to go to something easier. . . . The defendants protested loudly that it was the basis for their defense. . . . The execution appeared as predicted . . . on Channel 4, NBC, on the evening of January 27, 1981. The main defendant, Dr. Brady, appeared crest-fallen and thoroughly beaten. His sentence was death! The other defendant, Dr. Spence, didn't appear; therefore, he was let off with a suspended sentence with the rest of his life on good behavior. The Chief Magistrate proudly announced to the world that these two rascals were punished, and we need not fear them ever again.[6]

More substantively, however, Evans also put his finger on three major issues surrounding NEPEC: (1) appropriate "science court" processes, (2) selection of Council members from a pool, and (3) the increased probability of underground predictions. Evans argued as follows:

I would recommend that a "Code of Ethics" be established for persons serving as Council Members, and "Rules of Procedure" be established for the conduct of such meetings in the future. You also might wish to consider having a number of persons identified as Council Members in order to carefully select persons that have no personal or professional jealousy or antagonism toward a particular person. I fear that if our Council does not have some strict requirement, scientists in the future will be quite hesitant to appear or even to provide the results of their thinking.[7]

On January 30, 1981, CBS newsman Charles Osgood and the *Universe* crew spent four hours with Brady at the USBM research facility in Denver. Urged to do so by Chishing Wang (USBM–Washington), Brady wrote a short memo to Robert Marovelli describing the taping. He avoided criticizing NEPEC to the CBS crew, but he was clearly not ready to give up on his prediction:

The interview occupied approximately one-half day of my time and consisted of filming laboratory fracture of several rocks in our laboratory followed by an interview on the physical basis of the Peru prediction. The interview went very well. I was quite careful to avoid any potential controversy with the Geological Survey or with the "results" of the National Earthquake Prediction Evaluation Panel. The program will probably air sometime in June 1981, several

weeks prior to the first "predicted" event in central
Peru.

I will keep you informed on any new results relating to the prediction. Unfortunately, I am still convinced that the earthquakes will strike Peru later this year.[8]

Brady was correct about the CBS broadcast schedule. On June 23, 1981, Walter Cronkite's prime-time *Universe* did three stories. The middle feature, called "Quakecast," was devoted to the Brady-Spence prediction, especially Brady's appearance before NEPEC. At the conclusion, Charles Osgood asked Brady three pointed questions. It should be remembered that this exchange was taped only three days after the NEPEC meeting.

OSGOOD: Is this going to hurt you, though, as far as your career is concerned?

DR. BRADY: Absolutely. In—among my standing among my colleagues, absolutely. It has already. I just have to live with that.

OSGOOD: Would you evacuate Lima at this point?

DR. BRADY: Oh, I—that's not a subject for—that's a question I could never get involved in. That—that—these are political decisions.

OSGOOD: Well, let's put it another way. If you were in Lima at this point, what would you do?

DR. BRADY: What I would do personally? I wouldn't be in Lima at this particular point.

OSGOOD: Enough has transpired to make Brady believe the worst will still happen later this summer. Not enough has happened to make anyone else believe it. Even so, the prediction still stands and, within a few months, someone will be proven right and someone wrong.[9]

The very circumspect position taken by Brady after the NEPEC meeting reflected a USBM internal consensus developed just prior to the meeting. According to handwritten notes of a telephone conference call of January 23 between USBM–Washington and USBM–Denver officials, USBM would have no official position during or after the NEPEC meeting so as "not to embarrass USGS."[10] Following this up on February 5, after the NEPEC meetings, Chi-shing Wang in Robert Marovelli's office called Brady about how to relate to USGS. The main conclusion was that Brady should try to reroute IGP and U.S. Embassy–Lima requests for data interpretation to USGS for referral to Brady. According to Wang, Brady also "agreed to maintain low profile."[11]

If the NEPEC results (and procedures) generated qualms within USGS and USBM, they were even more pronounced at OFDA. Indeed, it was at this time, *after the NEPEC meeting*, that OFDA moved fully into the role of what might be called Brady's "bureaucratic champion." Moreover, it was not only Paul Krumpe who evinced doubts about NEPEC, but also his superior, Alan Van Egmond.

In early February, Krumpe offered a defense of Brady to his superiors. Again he highlighted the insurgent nature of the Brady approach: "Brady's current hypothesis appears unique in that it departs from accepted Einstein physics (Field Theory) and classical rock mechanics. He offers a comprehensive rational physical explanation for the following elements which, regardless of scale, contribute to lab rock failure, rock bursts and the occurrence of earthquakes."[12]

Krumpe went on to describe the NEPEC critiques of Brady during the two days of hearings and then summarized (side by side) the respective positions of Brady and

125

NEPEC on fourteen critical points. Krumpe did not really accept the NEPEC findings, and he noted the following:

> The National Earthquake Prediction Evaluation Council meeting resulted in a prepared statement to the Director of the USGS for subsequent transmittal to the President of Peru. The statement . . . apparently attempts to absolve the Council (and USGS), and the USG from further responsibility in all possible outcomes of the Brady prediction. *The statement of the Council rejecting the Brady hypothesis, Spence's plausibility arguments, and the deterministic sequence of events to possibly occur between now and summer 1981 remains inconclusive and subject to controversy.*[13]

Krumpe, who had obviously spoken with Brady, relayed the latter's perspective on the outcome of the NEPEC hearings:

> Dr. Brady's opinion of the meeting indicates that the NEPEC did not debunk or in any way scientifically discredit his theory, laboratory results or prediction with any valid argument, conclusion or evidence (data). Rather, the NEPEC persistently attempted to create a "smoke screen" during his presentation in order to obscure the fact that the Council, as constituted, was not capable of scientifically invalidating his conclusions and theory, even though he has published on the theoretical aspects, and his work was available to Council members prior to the meeting.[14]

Krumpe accepted Brady's contention that the prediction remained "on schedule" and recommended three OFDA actions: (1) support for periodic visits by NEPEC members or their consultants to Peru between May and September 1981 in order to assist the Peruvian government technically and "to provide a significant deterrent to fear during the times of the predicted earthquakes"; (2) assembly of a "Blue Ribbon" committee of international disaster experts to assess likely behavior in Peru between April and October 1981; and (3) upgrading of the IGP seismic detection network.[15]

In his own report to OFDA Director Mitchell, Van Egmond criticized NEPEC for its peremptory treatment of Brady and for what he saw as a lack of objectivity, but he also criticized Brady and Spence for lack of preparation and formal layout of theory and prediction:

> It is unrealistic to expect a panel, no matter how distinguished and unbiased, to scientifically assess and critique such a complex and intricate formulation in a day and a half, with little advance preparation. Also, it is unfortunate that many of the panel members have strong institutional and other ties (e.g. funding relationships, superior-subordinate relations) which could unduly affect the Council's deliberations.
>
> It is extremely unfortunate that Drs. Brady and Spence's formulations and findings during the past two years have not been set down in writing. It is incumbent on both persons to devote their full time and energies to accomplishing this task as an immediate priority.[16]

Van Egmond recommended to Mitchell that OFDA observe the NEPEC findings while taking advantage of "heightened local awareness of the earthquake hazard" to push preparedness in Peru and in the Andean region generally.[17]

With all of the publicity and the likelihood of continued bureaucratic conflict, higher USAID officials now became more involved. On February 19, Gordon Pierson, who supervised OFDA as well as other operations, wrote a quick "information memorandum" on the Brady-Spence prediction for the acting administrator of USAID. Interestingly, Pierson juxtaposed (1) the specific NEPEC judgment, (2) the general earthquake threat, (3) resultant OFDA program interests, and (4) a subtle jibe at NEPEC procedures:

> The National Earthquake Prediction Council found no specific basis for the Brady prediction but, of course, stated that a serious earthquake could occur in the region at any time. In this context, OFDA will be working with Peruvians to improve their preparedness for such a possibility.
>
> I propose to send copies of Alan Van Egmond's memo [critical of NEPEC] to LAC [USAID's Latin American Bureau], State and the USGS. As you will note, he accepts the Council's judgment, and we will be guided accordingly. However, the nature of the review was not what one would have wished and others should at least be aware of those reservations.[18]

On March 9, 1981, Pierson received a response from USAID Administrator M. Peter McPherson, who requested *another* information memorandum on "the nature of Peruvian and AID preparations in the event that there is an earthquake in June."[19] Krumpe and Van Egmond prepared a history of OFDA involvement in the Brady-Spence prediction and a status report for Pierson. Interestingly, the status report included the most recent dollar figures for the Carnegie/IGP proposal to upgrade the Peruvian seismic detection network:

	USG Contribution	GOP Contribution
FY 1981	$414,000	$250,000
FY 1982	$343,000	$209,000

Within USAID/OFDA, the Carnegie/IGP proposal was explained by the clear need to extend and improve Peru's

inadequate detection network. Krumpe, however, justified it to Van Egmond on the basis of an "early warning"
capability: "Earthquake disaster early warning is a real
possibility in Peru with the AutoSeis system. Given such
an interactive system Peruvian seismologists and Civil
Defense experts can effectively implement an early warning program and save thousands of lives. Such a system
is currently operational in California. This system could
be operational in Peru within 4–5 months. There are no
known technical delays to full implementation. This proposal is cost-effective indeed, given the magnitude of possible disaster now threatening Peru."[20]

This "early warning" argument is very strange indeed.
No one, in California or elsewhere, had ever claimed to
have an "operational" seismic detection early warning
system. *Only if one accepted Brady's theory* could any existing or proposed seismic detection system be conceived of
as allowing any kind of warning—early, late, or otherwise. That is, most geoscientists agree that interpretation
of earthquake patterns will probably be an important
component of any *future* prediction capability, but the
state of the art at that time was inadequate for prediction,
unless, of course, one accepted Brady's theory and allowed him to cluster and interpret seismicity in a region.
Krumpe apparently misunderstood the Carnegie/IGP proposal and overstated to his superiors the immediate lifesaving possibilities of a seismic detection network. At any
rate, on March 25, Gordon Pierson composed his formal
response to USAID Administrator McPherson. He noted
that USAID, the government of Peru, and international
organizations had undertaken preparation "in the event
there is an earthquake in June." Nonetheless, he noted
the following: "These measures are not being pursued in
the context of the Brady prediction, given the recent determination of the National Earthquake Prediction Evalu-

129

ation Council, but rather in the knowledge that Peru 'has experienced many strong earthquakes and others must be expected in the future both there and elsewhere along the coastal regions.' "[21]

Pierson continued by emphasizing (1) the damage implications of the Brady prediction, (2) the USAID administrator's stake in the case, and (3) the existing lack of consensus on how to respond: "There is general agreement that adequate planning for an earthquake of the magnitude of the Brady prediction probably is impossible. As the President's Special Coordinator for International Disaster Assistance, you should be aware, however, that there are varying views in the Office of U.S. Foreign Disaster Assistance (OFDA), the Latin American Bureau (LAC), the Department of State, and the US Geological Survey (USGS) on the nature and extent of the preparedness warranted in this instance."[22]

Pierson told McPherson that USAID disaster preparedness activities had not traditionally been a focus in mainline development planning but that OFDA had been active on its own. Pierson specifically mentioned the Carnegie/IGP proposal to upgrade Peru's "earthquake monitoring and early warning capabilities." Interestingly, this memo represents a double capture by staff of chiefs. Totally without background in the actual techniques of earthquake prediction and obviously without time to research the issue himself, Gordon Pierson accepted the "early warning capability" argument made by Krumpe. As staff to a higher chief, however, Pierson passed the argument along to USAID Administrator McPherson, capturing him.

Pierson concluded his memo to McPherson with a description of Peruvian government actions, and he again clearly reflected ambivalence about the Brady prediction:

Although the Brady prediction has been public knowledge in Peru for the past five years, public awareness has escalated sharply in the past 12 months. The GOP has long considered high earthquake vulnerability to be a very serious problem but is reluctant or unable to assign to it a high priority in a fiscal or developmental context. Peru recognizes that it is not well prepared for disasters, but fears that a highly visible preparedness effort would raise the anxiety level of an already-tense population. Peru's National Institute of Geophysics, although competently staffed is beset with budgetary and bureaucratic problems.[23]

In close contact with Brady in Colorado, Paul Krumpe began another series of internal OFDA memos on April 15, 1981. These memos were side-by-side comparisons of "Brady earthquake prediction statements" and "occurrence of events," but the arrangement and interpretation of events supported Brady's "prediction statements." Krumpe sent Van Egmond and Martin Howell an "update" on April 22. Again the tone and substance were supportive, but this time Krumpe offered a judgment:

The period 3/4/81 to 6/28/81 is a time when an increase in seismicity in the target zone (foreshocks) would tend to support Brady's prediction statements. Though not in the teleseismic range, events did occur on March 4, March 28, and April 10 at magnitude 4.0.

The attached Reuter News release indicates earthquakes occurred near Ayacucho, Peru, during the period April 18–20. The Peruvians have confirmed the dates and magnitudes of reported events. The magnitude range was 4.0–5.2. Some events were teleseismic. In my judgment, this series of earthquakes correlates with prediction statements made by Dr. Brady.[24]

In Peru: Concern and a "Second Evaluation"

Meanwhile, despite the NEPEC statement, anxiety continued to mount in Peru, and the U.S. Embassy in Lima called on John Filson to make good a promise to visit Peru—very publicly:

> Embassy hereby requests that Dr. John Filson of USGS, in coordination with AID/OFDA, travel to Lima in near future for discussions with Peruvian Geophysical Institute and Peruvian Civil Defense authorities concerning earthquake risk in general. As Department aware, predictions of Dr. Brian Brady that catastrophic earthquake is approaching continue to receive considerable press coverage. Embassy strongly believes that visit to Peru by Dr. Filson at this time would go long way to help allay public fear and put Brady's predictions in proper perspective.[25]

On April 28, Brady wrote directly to Alberto Giesecke in Lima (1) to apologize for giving some phone interviews to the Lima press, the substance of which was "distorted," (2) to express his gratitude for the seismicity data, but most importantly (3) to explain his evaluation of the current situation:

> I have been following the seismic situation in Peru carefully and the addition of the local data has been invaluable. I have been studying the local network data, and at this time, there have been a total of nine events (magnitudes 3.8–4.5) in the nucleation zone.

With the exception of the December 26, 1980, event (M 4.5), all the remaining events are below the teleseismic detection threshold. I have stated repeatedly in both memoranda and privately that the magnitudes of the "foreshocks" could not be predicted in advance. Local data is essential to accomplish this task. However, it appears to me at this time that the final active foreshock phase to the June 28, 1981, event (± several days) began on August 14, 1980 (M = 4.0). If the June event (M ≃ 8.2–8.4) occurs, the other events (M 9.2, M 9.9+) will follow. If this event does not occur, *I will withdraw the prediction.*[26]

That is, Brady maintained that his prediction was still correct. His interpretation of the data convinced him that the first great earthquake was coming on June 28. Cutting the other way, however, Brady noted that if the June 28 event failed to occur, then the entire prediction sequence should be ignored. Obviously, this April 28 letter put Giesecke, IGP, and the Peruvian government in a very difficult position. The NEPEC evaluation was negative, but Brady was positive. The acid test, however, was a great earthquake in sixty days.

Probably anticipating the thoroughly negative NEPEC evaluation of the Brady-Spence prediction, Giesecke had not attended the January 26–27 meetings. On April 2, 1981, however, Giesecke wrote to Dr. Roger Guerra-Garcia, president of the Consejo Nacional de Investigación (a Peruvian National Science Foundation). Citing a published article by John Roberts, a New Zealand professor of public administration who had attended the Brady-Spence meeting with President Belaúnde back in October 1980, Giesecke suggested that Guerra-Garcia solicit an evaluation of the prediction *from CERESIS.*[27] Technically, the request would have to be routed through Ramon

Cabré, S.J., president of the Consejo Directivo (a board of directors) of CERESIS, in La Paz, Bolivia. It should be remembered that CERESIS is headquartered in Lima, Alberto Giesecke was the director, and the original Roberts article appeared in *Revista Geofísica*, whose editorial board was headed at that time by . . . Alberto Giesecke.

Roger Guerra-Garcia did request this second evaluation, and on May 18, 1981, Father Cabré replied. The Cabré letter is a complicated three pages long. The first page recapped worldwide experience with earthquake predictions, noting that only a few had been accurate. Cabré also reviewed the details of the prediction for Peru. The centerpiece of the second page was a long quote (in English) from the NEPEC statement. The letter noted, however, that "some are of the opinion that when treating such an original theory [NEPEC] should have studied more deeply the foundation of the prediction."[28]

The Cabré letter went on to quote the Brady letter of April 28 and reiterated the need for a much improved seismic detection network in Peru and in the Andean area generally. Cabré then summarized the situation as follows:

1. The prediction for a pair of (great) earthquakes off the coast of Lima exists.
2. The magnitudes have been exaggerated.
3. "Scientists and . . . the authorities have studied the case and treated it with appropriate circumspection."
4. The mass media have exacerbated the public tension and given rise to anxiety.[29]

Guerra-Garcia prepared a report for President Belaúnde based on the letter from Father Cabré. Dated May 22, 1981, this letter pointed out that the Brady-Spence prediction was *scientific*, not the result of astrology or psychic insight. The letter noted, however, that "the Brady model is not accepted by the majority of Peruvian and foreign seismologists," and that it was not yet of proven worth.[30] The letter then suggested that reducing public tension was the most important immediate task.

Well-informed sources indicate that this bland, rather equivocal letter passed across Belaúnde's desk generating "neither pain nor glory." For the record, however, this second evaluation was much less harsh toward Brady and concentrated more on prediction *effects* than did the NEPEC statement.

In the U.S.

On May 7, 1981, Brady prepared a seventeen-page memo for his Bureau of Mines superiors in Denver and for Robert Marovelli in Washington. The memo, entitled "Status Report of Peru Earthquake Predictions," provided Brady's detailed interpretation of the 1980–81 seismicity patterns in central Peru. This memo is exceptionally well written and clear. In it Brady evinced no doubt about the continued viability of his theory and the accuracy of his prediction (the date changed again, however):

> I believe that the overall characteristics of the final foreshock phase are occurring as I had indicated to you in previous memoranda. The average magnitudes of these events is M = 4.0, approximately one-half magnitude unit below teleseismic detectability. A "rule of thumb" for estimating the magnitude of the first decoupling event is to add 4.1–4.3 units to the average foreshock magnitude to obtain the mag-

nitude of the mainshock. Application of this rule suggests the first event, tentatively predicted for July 6, 1981, will be of magnitude M = 8.1–8.3.[31]

Brady went on to explain the basics of his theoretical model, and he did so more precisely and concisely than he had either at the NEPEC hearings or at any other time:

The essential elements of the theory are as follows: A nucleation zone develops in a material prior to the occurrence of a phase change or, in our case, a failure or earthquake. The presence of this zone controls the behavior of material in its immediate vicinity. That is, the material undergoes cooperative motion which is occurring in response to any changes occurring within the nucleation zone. Thus, matter outside this zone can be said to have "knowledge" of the existence of this zone. The range of this cooperative motion is a function both of the time interval between its formation and the final failure and also of the energy required to complete the process. Thus, the greater the energy required, the greater the range and usually, though not necessarily, the time required to complete the failure preparation process. Because fracture is a local phenomenon (see, for example, *Theory of Earthquakes, Part I*, for experimental confirmation) any realistic description of the physics of fracture must necessarily be a local field theory with the additional complication that the theory describe a *local* second-order tensor field. The field equations I have developed are similar in form to the Einstein equations except with a different coupling constant between the geometrical description of the field and the energy momentum tensor. Solutions of the simplified equations predict the existence of a nucleation zone prior to the occurrence of the failure. The zone does not form instantaneously but rather evolves over its lifetime. A more correct description would be the zone "condenses out" within its environment and begins its evolutionary process of growth followed by eventual collapse. Collapse of the zone signals the occurrence of the mainshock (failure).[32]

Brady also included in his memo a pointed dig at "the seismological community":

Many within the seismological community are currently infatuated with simple fault models made more complex by the addition of asperities (hard zones along the fault surface) which tend to inhibit free body motion along the fault; an earthquake occurs once the asperities are broken. Thus, one "gets out" only what one "puts in"—in my opinion, a most unsatisfying state of affairs. I believe we need to address the fundamental problem of *how* the fault gets there in the first place. My theory does exactly this and, in addition, predicts the existence of a preparatory phase prior to the fractures. The Bureau's experience in rock bursts, where new faults are induced by the mining process, show dramatically that precursory effects, similar to those reported prior to some earthquakes, precede rock bursts. As you are aware, many of these bursts have been predicted prior to their occurrence.[33]

At about this time OFDA did a most remarkable thing. Despite the NEPEC evaluation, despite all of the criticism directed at them, OFDA invited Brady to visit Washington and present "his current interpretation and analysis of recent Peruvian seismicity."[34] OFDA also scheduled Brady to meet with various USAID officials. As Krumpe explained to OFDA Director Martin Howell on May 8: "The purpose of the meeting on May 13 is to allow Dr. Brady the opportunity to present and discuss his prediction, its possible implications, and provide evidence of its probable occurrence. The morning of May 14 (Thursday) is scheduled for additional discussion with you, the AID Administrator, and others as appropriate."[35]

The May 13 meeting gave Brady several hours to explain his model and prediction. At least twenty people attended, representing a variety of federal agencies, the Carnegie Institution, and Washington-area consulting firms. The main upshot of the meeting was a memorandum from USAID Administrator McPherson to *the secretary of state*, Alexander Haig. This memo portrayed Brady in a favorable light and mentioned the USGS/NEPEC position only once:

> Dr. Brian Brady, a research physicist with the U.S. Bureau of Mines, has predicted a series of great earthquakes to occur off the coast of Peru this summer. Based on available data, Dr. Brady contends that the first event will occur near Lima on or about July 6. Earthquakes of catastrophic magnitude, affecting the entire Pacific region, are predicted to follow in mid-August and late September. Dr. Brady's prediction technique is based on many years of research in the Department of Interior, Mine Safety program. He has successfully predicted mine collapse (small earthquakes) in the northern United States with the saving of many lives. In discussions with the Agency for International Development (AID), Dr. Brady explained the prediction technique and provided . . . [a] memorandum . . . to update his Peru prediction. The discussions were attended by the U.S. Geological Survey, Carnegie Institute of Washington, Federal

Emergency Management Agency, Bureau of Mines, Agency for International Development, and State representatives. The U.S. Geological Survey and the National Earthquake Prediction Evaluation Council have formally rejected Dr. Brady's theory and its application in the Peru prediction. Nevertheless, AID is monitoring the prediction as a necessary part of its disaster contingency planning responsibility. The cooperation of the U.S. Embassy in Peru has been outstanding and I am most appreciative.[36]

That is, this case had reached about as high a level as a non-national-security matter could go, the secretary of state. Moreover, it seems clear that the chiefs (OFDA Director Howell and USAID Administrator McPherson) had been captured by their staff. McPherson's memo to Secretary of State Haig is another classic example. McPherson spends most of his time on the prediction, Brady's background, and the attention given the prediction. He slips in the NEPEC evaluation at the end but immediately dilutes it with a "nevertheless" statement.

This may well be the greatest danger when a scientific controversy becomes highly politicized: the chiefs in the game, the real heavyweights, are not scientists and are therefore vulnerable to having staff put words in their mouths, or worse yet, in their memos. The capture becomes complete if the chief has only *internal* (intra-agency) documents to read. Whoever finally wrote the McPherson memo to Haig certainly did not have (or at least use) any USGS documents.

139

NINE

"Doomsday" Approaches
—and Passes

Another Date Change

Around the time of the May 13 meeting, Brady again changed the projected date for the first major earthquake, from June 28 to June 14. When apprised of this, Peruvian Civil Defense Director Edmundo Masias contacted the U.S. Embassy in Lima in an attempt to advance the dates of John Filson's symbolically important visit. The Embassy cabled Washington: "Admiral Edmundo Masias, head of Peruvian Civil Defense (CD) has requested that John Filson's travel to Peru, which we understand is being programmed for June 26 to July 1, be moved forward to the end of May. This would allow CD and other Peruvian authorities to consult with Filson and to maximize the impact of visit to calm apprehensions of public about the earthquake series predicted by USBM scientist Dr. Brian Brady to hit Lima on June 28."[1]

This exchange is significant because it demonstrates that both the U.S. and the Peruvian governments knew of the Brady date change. This information was never divulged to the public, however, and June 28 remained the date of attention for the Peruvian people.

An Adviser/Observer in Lima

Paul Flores, a disaster preparedness specialist from California and member of the UNDRO/OFDA-sponsored team which visited Peru in January 1981, was contracted by OFDA to assist the Peruvian government, specifically Civil Defense, in the key period from late May to late July 1981. Flores worked out of Peruvian Civil Defense and was mandated to (1) prepare and help carry out a communications simulation exercise across the various Peruvian ministries, (2) develop a general earthquake response plan for metropolitan Lima, (3) execute a comprehensive simulation exercise to evaluate the Lima earthquake response plan, (4) estimate the resource needs for responding to an earthquake disaster affecting metropolitan Lima, and (5) assist international organizations and private voluntary agencies in their response planning.

As an outside expert temporarily located in a key government agency during a crucial period, Flores was in a unique position to observe Peruvian responses to the Brady-Spence prediction. His principal observations were as follows:[2]

1. The prediction was a pervasive topic of conversation all over Lima and at every level of society. Media coverage was intense, and informal leaflets about earthquakes, disasters in general, and "what to do" were everywhere.

2. In addition to seeking support and assistance from

141

the U.S. and international organizations, Peruvian experts and government officials also turned to the Japanese, with a special eye on the "countermeasures" program adopted in the Tokai area southwest of Tokyo.

3. The press, government officials, and the general public blamed a marked drop in foreign tourism on the prediction.

4. Peruvian Civil Defense was "totally overwhelmed" by requests for information and presentations on earthquakes and earthquake protection by other government agencies, private companies, banks, hotels, and citizen groups. They could respond to only about ten percent of the requests.

5. The June 11, 1981, communications exercise demonstrated that hardware shortages and incompatibility made Civil Defense coordination of the multiministry response highly problematic. Even the U.S. Embassy could not communicate with Peruvian Civil Defense. Moreover, an engineering evaluation of the ability of the Civil Defense building itself to withstand a major earthquake "was not favorable."

6. A general response plan for the Lima metropolitan area was prepared and submitted to President Belaúnde, his cabinet, and the National Defense Council. It was approved, in part because it is the "responsibility of the President to decide whether or not the armed forces will take control of the emergency. . . . The fact that Civil Defense has a specific plan may influence . . . that final decision."[3] That is, the last thing that President Belaúnde wanted was the military back out of the barracks to "take control of the emergency," any emergency.

7. The July 14, 1981, simulation exercise of the Lima metropolitan earthquake response plan demonstrated that despite considerable improvement, Peruvian Civil Defense still had major organizational problems:

he has. However, I reluctantly have concluded that he believes too much in the correctness of the prediction of the Peru earthquakes to function self-critically in assessing the relevant seismic data."[8]

In the Agencies

As the predicted dates neared and as the pressure and anxiety mounted, Paul Krumpe prepared another "prediction update" for OFDA Director Howell and Van Egmond. On June 12, Krumpe argued that Brady had "predicted" several of the smaller events in the target zone prior to their occurrence over the previous several months. He also passed along other evidence, but there was a note of desperation:

> Other information which may tend to corroborate Brady's "preferred" time for the first event include: 1) an apparent abnormal increase in the presence of fleas in Lima. This occurrence was observed in Arica in 1868 just prior to a large (M = 9.0) earthquake on August 8. 2) ants have been reported swarming out of the ground during the last few days (it is the dormant season, winter, in Peru). 3) within the target zone seismicity appears to be very low in magnitude and frequency, however, along the boundary of the primary aftershock zone (inland up and down the coast) a *significant* increase in teleseismic events began the first week in June. This appears consistent with statements made by Dr. Brady in his recent memo (May 7).[9]

Brady prepared a status report of his own for the USBM leadership. In this June 19 memo, Brady reverted to a

June 26–30, 1981, time window for his "first event": "I believe at this time that the first event in central Peru will occur between June 26 and June 30, 1981. This latest revision is based on the addition of data obtained recently from the Peruvian local network."[10] At the same time, however, he also laid the groundwork for a retraction: "If the first mainshock does not occur by June 30, 1981, I must conclude that my interpretation of space time seismicity patterns in central Peru is in error and, accordingly, the probability of the occurrence of the predicted earthquakes in Peru this summer will be lessened considerably. If the first event does not occur by July 10, 1981, I will formally withdraw the prediction and will prepare a statement to be transmitted to Dr. Alberto Giesecke on that date."[11]

Meanwhile, the Carnegie/IGP proposal to fund the major renovation of the Peruvian seismic network was encountering bureaucratic opposition. USAID–Washington official for Latin America Edward Coy initially *opposed* the Carnegie/IGP funding proposal. In a June 22 memo to OFDA Director Howell, Coy noted that at the end of a February 1981 meeting with Krumpe, Van Egmond, and Howell, he thought that "there was a consensus that the proposal was not appropriate for AID funding." Coy was concerned that the $750,000 would set a precedent and "generate many requests from similar institutions around the world." Coy also noted the potential public-relations problems inherent in the proposal: "In view of the sad history of the Brady affair, singling out Peru for an equipment project only tends to reopen a controversy we have been trying to close."[12]

As "the Brady affair" moved toward the critical date of June 28, strain between agencies became even clearer. On June 24, Krumpe attempted to send a cable to the U.S. Embassy in Lima which was, in effect, the internal USBM memo of June 19 from Brady to his superiors. The USAID desk officer cleared the cable, but the State Department desk officer, John Andrew Purnell, absolutely refused. Purnell later explained his position: "If that message had been leaked, the fact that the statement was only contained in an internal Bureau of Mines memorandum would have been immaterial to the Peruvian press, which would have played it with large, front page headlines as an official document setting forth the position of the U.S. government."[13]

In a fascinating aside, Purnell also explained why he preferred telephone contact with Lima to letter or cable exchanges. He "assumed the Peruvian Government was monitoring the conversations," and he "wanted them to know that the doubts [he] was casting on the Brady case to the Peruvian Embassy in Washington were exactly the same line [he] was taking with [U.S. Embassy] people in Lima."[14]

On June 24, 1981, Krumpe responded to Coy. In a memo to Van Egmond, Krumpe did not recall any consensus on not funding the Carnegie/IGP proposal. Indeed, as Krumpe remembered it, "at no time during the meeting or in subsequent meetings . . . was it the stated position of the [USAID Latin American] Bureau that this program should *not* be funded with OFDA disaster preparedness funds."[15] Nonetheless, it was OFDA Director Howell's position that OFDA would not fund the Carnegie/IGP proposal "without full concurrence from the U.S. Geological Survey, the [USAID Latin American] Bureau, and State Peru Desk."[16]

Because the proposal involved only OFDA money and did not require any supplement from USAID Latin American Bureau funds, Coy ultimately acquiesced to the Carnegie/IGP program. Purnell recalled how the State Department concurrence and that of USGS came about:

Toward the end of my time on the Peru desk, I believe late July of 1981, I recall meeting with John Filson and the then director of OFDA, a Reagan administration appointee and retired colonel. Dr. Filson had originally dismissed the proposal as ludicrous, saying Giesecke would be getting a Cadillac, a more elaborate system than most U.S. universities have. . . . The retired colonel . . . openly admitted that *if we opposed the expenditure they would quickly have to find some other way to obligate the funds.* After further discussion, investigation and reflection, Filson and I agreed not to oppose OFDA's proposal.[17]

The Day: June 28, 1981

John Filson made his requested visit to Lima and was visibly present (press conferences, TV appearances) during the critical prediction window, the days surrounding June 28.

Nothing happened.

On July 2, 1981, the U.S. Embassy in Lima sent an unclassified cable to Washington. The title was "The Earthquake That Wasn't":

1. SUMMARY: The population of Lima passed a quiet Sunday, 28 June, the date most widely believed to be that predicted by Brian Brady of the U.S. Bureau of Mines for a large earthquake to hit the city. Media coverage of the palliative statements by President Belaunde in visiting coastal Pisco (near the predicted epicenter), on June 28, by Dr. John Filson of the U.S. Geological Survey visiting Lima, and by the Chiefs of Civil Defense and the

Peruvian Geophysical Institute helped to take most of the voltage out of the somewhat charged atmosphere in the capital city. With the 28th "safely" past, the media are now happily burying the Brady prediction. End summary.

2. Since Feb. 1980, knowledge of the prediction by Dr. Brian Brady of the U.S. Bureau of Mines of a series of earthquakes to strike Lima, culminating in a once in 800,000 year jolt of 9.9 on the Richter scale, has caused varying amounts of anxiety among the local populace. Working from a continuous flow of seismic information from Peru, early on, Dr. Brady fixed on June 28 as the likely date for the first of these shocks. Although he had shifted the predicted date several times since, the 28th was the date which received early and broad publicity and on which believers in the prediction and skeptics alike fixed their attention.

3. The visit of Dr. John Filson, Chief of the Office of Earthquake Prediction [sic] of the U.S. Geological Survey, from June 25 through 29 proved most useful. His stay was highlighted by two press conferences devoted almost entirely to questions about the Brady prediction. Front-page treatment was given by the media to Dr. Filson's reiteration at those conferences of the U.S. National Earthquake Prediction Evaluation Council's rejection of the Brady prediction.

4. Peruvian authorities were also active in publicly rejecting the Brady prediction, and in terms more unequivocal than previously. The chief of the prestigious Peruvian Geophysical Institute spoke out against the scientific validity of the Brady theory and the Institute's scientific director of seis-

mology denied that recent earthquakes in the southern mountains of Peru (Ayacucho) had anything to do with the Brady prediction.

5. The most prominent public statement against the Brady prediction was that of President Belaunde. The president claimed to the media that a trip he was making on the 28th to Pisco to dedicate the La Puntilla fish freezing and canning plant and other public works was being undertaken in defiance of Brady's prediction of the earthquake epicentered in the sea to the west of that town. The president's gesture came in neat counterpoint to the Air Force's quietly pulling their planes out of the low-lying sea front airbase at Pisco (at which the Belaunde party landed). The Air Force apparently had misread the prediction to include a 60 foot tsunami (tidal wave) at the time of the predicted first mainshock. The Air Force was not alone in its miscue. The country's first census in many years was postponed from the 28th in part to avoid the predicted earthquake.

6. The reaction to the passing of the predicted day has been one of relief and exhilaration, best typified by the June 29 *Expreso* headline: "Peru, Si! Brady, No!" Some inquiries have been made regarding when Dr. Brady will retract his prediction, but the general feeling is that the fact that no earthquake occurred on the twenty-eighth ended the affair. The retraction will be welcome when it may come but its reception here is likely to be distinctly less than earthshaking.[18]

Upon his return from Lima, Filson wrote a trip report to the chief geologist and the director of USGS. His first point focused on the impact of the prediction in Lima:

First, I had no idea of the level of anxiety and concern these predictions had caused in Lima. During my stay, every newspaper contained at least one front page story about Brady; property values have fallen drastically in Lima; many who could afford it left town for the weekend, and the people at the hotel where I stayed said their bookings were down to about one-third normal. . . . The Department of the Interior continues to look foolish in that it allows these predictions to be promulgated and revised periodically while the Director of the Survey and the Prediction Evaluation Council have denied unconditionally the validity of the predictions.[19]

Neatly reflecting scientific reservations about Brady's theory overlaid on bureaucratic and organizational concerns, Filson made his second point:

Secondly, I am concerned about the effects of Brady's prediction on legitimate earthquake prediction research conducted in the Survey. If one accepts Brady's theories, one has to reject the second law of thermodynamics and other widely accepted physical principles. We can say with confidence that Brady is wrong, but we cannot say that there will not be a major earthquake in Lima this summer. . . . Brady has revised his prediction at least three times since May, moving the probable date of the first event up to June 10 and recently back to July 10. If he is allowed to continue to play this game of roulette, he will eventually get a hit and his theories will be considered valid by many. If it is assumed by Congress, Administration officials, or the public that Brady has solved the earthquake prediction problem, major difficulties for our current efforts could ensue.[20]

Filson concluded by referencing Brady's June 19 memo offering to withdraw his prediction if the first earthquake failed to materialize by July 10. Filson urged that "steps be taken through the Department [of the Interior] to ensure that Brady honors his most recent pledge to withdraw his predictions."[21] Actually, this was unnecessary, because Brady was then attempting to do exactly that.

Brady Withdraws

On July 9, 1981, Brady prepared a draft letter to Alberto Giesecke withdrawing his prediction, but the inclusion of the final sentence would delay the letter more than a week:

> I believe that my prediction of large seismic events off the coast of central Peru as originally stated at the NEPEC meeting in late January 1981 is incorrect. At this meeting I introduced the possibility of an event to occur on or about June 28, 1981, off the coast of central Peru and that this event would initiate the decoupling process between the Nazca and South American plates. Without the occurrence of this event I judge the probability of the occurrence of the two remaining large events to be exceedingly low. . . . I am relieved that circumstances now suggest that my interpretation of the space time seismicity patterns in central Peru is incorrect. I will correspond with you in more detail in the near future.[22]

Brady's superiors in Washington would not clear the letter if it contained any reference to future correspondence, and the last sentence was deleted. Brady's letter (without the last sentence) was sent on July 20. On July 29, the deputy director of USBM did respond to USGS, however, and he indicated that the Brady letter had been "in process" most of the month. He could not resist a small jab at USGS as well:

As you are aware the Bureau of Mines did not take an official position in this matter since we neither had the official responsibility in this area nor the technical expertise. We did not constrain Dr. Brady from responding to requests for information since he has a demonstrated record of scientific accomplishment and we continue to feel he is a responsible and competent scientist. Similarly, we never questioned the professional competence of Dr. William Spence of the USGS when he initially was supportive of Dr. Brady and more recently when he withdrew that support.[23]

Final Bitterness

If Brady's withdrawal of his prediction was the climax of this case, then there was a two-part denouement: (1) the funding of the Carnegie/IGP proposal, and (2) what might be called "the Krumpe flap." On the first issue, out of its own disaster preparedness funds, OFDA obligated $784,608 for fiscal years 1981–83 to completely upgrade the seismic detection network for the general Lima area. The second issue arose when Clarence Allen of Cal Tech, chairman of NEPEC, wrote a blistering letter to USAID Administrator McPherson, with copies to all the members of NEPEC, the U.S. ambassador to Peru, the director of USGS, the president of the National Academy of Sciences, and Brian Brady and Paul Krumpe themselves.

Writing as professor at Cal Tech and as chairman of NEPEC, Allen wanted to "express . . . dismay at the activities of the Agency for International Development during this tragic episode."[24] Specifically, Allen excoriated Krumpe:

> Acting against the advice of virtually every seismologist in the United States, the Agency for International Development appears to have continued to put credence in the Brady prediction, bringing great and unnecessary trauma to the Peruvian people and considerable frivolous expense to the American taxpayer. This seems to have come about because one of your staff members, Mr. Paul Krumpe of OFDA, has taken it upon himself not only to embrace the Brady prediction, but actually to aid and abet Dr. Brady in its promulgation. I use the words "aid and abet" advisedly, as a result of having observed Mr. Krumpe at an international earthquake-prediction meeting in Argentina last October and at the meeting of our National Earthquake Prediction Evaluation Council in January, as well as having heard of his various other activities here and in Peru. He has clearly been unwilling to accept the unanimous recommendation of the scientists on the Evaluation Council—which was set up specifically to advise federal agencies on such problems—and he seems to have gone his own way without effective guidance from his supervisors in your own Agency.[25]

Allen argued that Brady's hypothesis lacked peer support, that Spence had defected in June, but that Krumpe appeared undeterred—despite a lack of geophysics credentials. Interestingly, Allen himself noted the paradigm-challenge aspects of the case:

> Mr. Krumpe seems to have perceived his proper role as one of protecting the brilliant, young martyr from the big, bad scientific establishment. It is indeed true

that a number of important scientific discoveries have resulted from hypotheses that were broadly criticized at the time, and earth scientists in particular can point to several such episodes. But is it really appropriate for the Agency for International Development, with its very limited scientific expertise, to be involved in such a scenario, particularly when it is the people of a foreign country who are the innocent "guinea pigs" involved?[26]

Allen recognized that the NEPEC hearings were "not above criticism," and he even evinced some sympathy for Brady—but not for Krumpe:

Much as I disagree with Dr. Brady's scientific (and social) judgment, I find his behavior easier to understand than that of your Mr. Krumpe. Dr. Brady has reasonable scientific credentials and has considerable experience in rock-mechanics studies that are relevant to earthquakes, and I can understand his zeal to make a significant scientific breakthrough—however misguided this particular effort may have been. But Mr. Krumpe's primary obligations, it seems to me, are to serve his Agency and the American people in giving the best possible scientific advice on problems related to foreign disasters. Instead of doing this in a reasonably professional and dispassionate way, he has chosen to become himself the enthusiastic advocate of a highly debatable hypothesis—and he has evidently carried along others in the Agency with him. I find the whole episode almost incredible.[27]

The formal response to Allen's July 10, 1981, letter came on July 22, and it was written by OFDA Director Howell. He reminded Allen that (1) it was USAID that had funded John Filson's trip to Lima; (2) USBM had allowed Brady to continue work on the predictions after the

NEPEC meetings; and (3) the U.S. Embassy in Lima had continued to ask Brady for his analyses of seismic data for their conversations with IGP. Howell then explicitly defended Krumpe: "Under these circumstances, AID would have been remiss in not remaining informed until the prediction was withdrawn by Dr. Brady. Mr. Krumpe had the task of gathering this information. He is a loyal and dedicated officer who was seeking to keep AID advised under very difficult circumstances."[28]

Perhaps more important than his defense of a single individual, however, was Howell's explication of USAID/OFDA activities in general. The OFDA director neatly captured the essence of the bureaucratic dilemma of being caught between organizational needs and the scientific judgment of NEPEC:

> The Agency for International Development supported the Council's review of the Brady prediction and abided by its findings. At the same time, AID continued to respond to requests for assistance from the Government of Peru in seismic detection, disaster preparedness, and contingency planning on the basis of the recommendations of the U.S. Embassy and AID mission there. This was not done to lend credence to the Brady prediction, but to fulfill AID's Congressional mandate to help countries save lives. It would have been unacceptable for AID to wait several months until the Brady prediction had passed before continuing these projects. However, AID was careful to emphasize that its focus was directed toward the chronic earthquake hazard which confronts Peru and not the Brady prediction.[29]

Ultimately, USAID and OFDA received letters and cables supporting Krumpe from a variety of sources: Alberto Giesecke in Peru, Alford Cooley of the U.S. Embassy in Lima, and Ambassador Corr himself. A letter from Giesecke was most laudatory. On January 11, 1982, Giesecke wrote to OFDA Director Howell commending Krumpe's "dedication and interest" and acknowledging that Krumpe's support for the IGP/Carnegie proposal had been central to its approval. About the Brady affair, Giesecke noted that one seldom "finds [a] government functionary so keenly dedicated to support basic activities . . . essential for the understanding of the mechanisms which cause disasters."[30] From all appearances, Krumpe's career was undamaged. Indeed, he was promoted in 1982. In both 1982 and 1983, USAID nominated Krumpe for the congressional Excalibur Award.

It might be fitting here to offer a note on William Spence, whose career was damaged. In November 1981, Alberto Giesecke wrote to John Filson in an attempt to obtain USGS–Reston approval for Spence (who was "reluctant") to participate in a postmortem study of the case. Filson responded that Spence was busy on "new and interesting problems these days" and that he should focus on this new work. Filson then laid out the "real" reason for restricting Spence's participation in anything related to the Brady affair: "It is unlikely that Bill's travel to Peru will be approved by the Survey regardless of the source of funding for the project. Indeed, I would be reluctant to forward such a request given the occurrences during his visit to Lima last time and the major difficulties that ensued for this Office and the Geological Survey. Thus, if Bill wants to contribute to the project I am afraid it must be through the mails."[31]

For his part, Brian Brady continued his mine safety work at USBM, but he also ("on his own time") reworked the mathematical calculations for the Peru earthquake sequence. Over the next several years he offered at least one more specific prediction for Lima, but this was kept between Brady, OFDA in Washington, and Alberto Gie-secke in Lima. That is, for a time Brady did not give up on his *theory*, admitting only that his *mathematics* was in error. His "hit" never came, however, and Brady gradu-ally lost interest in trying to recalculate his prediction.

The battle was over.

TEN

Reflections

Our narrative of the Brady-Spence earthquake prediction controversy may be over, but this book is not. The problem is how to conclude the study. It turns out that fighting one's way through a thicket of trees does not necessarily yield a good perspective on the forest. Indeed, it may well be that the authors of a close empirical study are the least able to draw general conclusions. This sense of limitation was reinforced by the fact that virtually every colleague who read our drafts wished to take generalization in a different direction. Therefore, staying relatively close to the material, we would simply like to offer some reflections and attempt to answer the broad questions posed by Kuhn and Blissett as they apply to this particular controversy.

In truth, the preceding eight chapters were both very easy and terribly difficult to write. They were easy in the sense that at a certain point, a good story begins to tell itself, and the authors become a vehicle for the exposition. At the same time, chronicling the evolution of the Brady-Spence controversy was difficult because of the strain imposed by the effort to be both understanding and objective.

159

Real politics are intensely personal, and the individuals involved in the Brady-Spence affair retain painful memories to this day. Moreover, all of the major participants are alive, and most have continuing careers in the same agencies as in 1980–81. Only Robert Marovelli at USBM and Alberto Giesecke at IGP have retired. Therefore, telling the story entailed a special responsibility. To attempt to understand the individuals, their actions, and their motives, we often had to project ourselves "inside" the participants, but without identifying with them. That is, we had to be able to empathize with the individuals involved without crossing the line into personal sympathy or antipathy. Agonizing over multiple drafts became a necessary ordeal. In fact, we now better understand the attractions of quantitative research.

The Individuals

Perhaps the most important lesson we should draw here is also the most human: the entire experience was very hard on the individuals. There is no escaping the fact that at least for John Filson, Alberto Giesecke, Robert Marovelli, and Paul Krumpe, as well as for Brian Brady and William Spence, the prediction, and what to do with and about it, occupied hundreds of personal and professional hours. Indeed, for several, the prediction controversy dominated their lives for the better part of two years. As we hope the preceding chapters have made clear, each person was "trying to do the right thing," or at least trying not to do the wrong thing, but different jobs in different organizations meant very different definitions of "the right thing." Complicating the decision-making environment were the high scientific uncertainty surrounding the prediction and the terrible implications if the prediction turned out to be correct. Of course, as we have seen, the effects of a wrong prediction were not inconsequential either.

In sum, all of the participants were torn in various directions, and there were no clear winners. Indeed, as one said, "we all lost, some more than others, but we all lost." As an overall statement, that is a sobering observation.

Challenge and Control

As noted in Chapter I, Thomas Kuhn and Marlan Blissett wanted to know more about how modern scientific communities handle challenges to orthodoxy, "impermissible aberrations," especially when they turn out to be failures. The Brady-Spence prediction obviously qualifies on both counts, as a bold challenge and ultimately a failure. To be fair, however, it appears that Brian Brady and especially William Spence did not set out to challenge directly the fundamental plate tectonic paradigm of geology/seismology. In fact, they worked within the plate tectonic paradigm and even within the seismic gap approach to earthquake prediction. What really set them at odds with the vast majority of their peers was the argument that Brady's deterministic model was the "puzzle-solver" that would leap over the slow, incremental, cautious work of most scientists and proceed directly to specific (date, place, magnitude) earthquake predictions. In a restricted sense, the Brady model was threatening because it implied a whole new research tradition based on laboratory experiments, and research support to the seismological research community would have been completely realigned had Brady proved correct.

The issue of funding is critical. Direct and indirect government support obviously defines the scope, direction, and pace of modern scientific inquiry. Given the important role of science in national development and international competition, scientists must be willing to fight for what they believe in. It is time to recognize, however, that because government dominates the funding of modern science, conflicts between scientists will often become overtly bureaucratic in nature, especially when the stakes are high. In future studies of scientific controversies, analysis should start, not conclude, with the bureaucratic politics of science. Indeed, if this book accomplishes nothing else, it should destroy once and for all the myth that scientists are apolitical. In the pursuit of truth but also in the pursuit of grants, contracts, research programs, travel, and prestige, scientists play politics—by necessity.

If "bureaucratically" is one part of the answer to the Kuhn/Blissett question about how scientific communities handle challenges to orthodoxy, the second part of the answer revolves around the concept of escalating stages of control. An important initial question in any scientific controversy is whether the scientific establishment attempts to actively "control" an impermissible aberration or whether it simply lets the unorthodox idea run its course and fade away. That is, it is very difficult for anything but an incremental within-paradigm step to obtain a full and constructive hearing. Mere publication in some journal is never enough. A novel theory or approach must be recognized, cited, and *used* by peers ("converts") and students to perpetuate itself. Otherwise, it dies out.

We saw that although Brady published his articles between 1974 and 1976, he converted (temporarily) only William Spence. Moreover, as a U.S. government research scientist, Brady had little access to trainable graduate students. Brady's complaint was that he "never received a response" to his ideas, even from NEPEC. It took other players (Spence, Pakiser, Giesecke, and Krumpe) to obtain audiences for Brady. Even then, very few scientists said anything, and criticism was muted, at least until the NEPEC meeting.

Therefore, neglect appears to be the first-level response by the scientific establishment to unorthodoxy. If attention to the novelty is then forced, "passive control" (polite hearing, but no response) is the second step. "Active control" (threats, sanctions, rewards, attacks) comes later, partly because most incipient challenges fail to survive neglect and passive control, partly because active control requires the expenditure of that scarcest of all resources for scientists, time. The question then becomes, what pushes or pulls a controversy past neglect and polite (in)attention?

In the case of the Brady-Spence controversy, three factors stand out: (1) action-agency involvement, (2) media coverage, and (3) a divided, intellectually insecure scientific community.

The involvement in the Brady-Spence affair of USAID's Office of Foreign Disaster Assistance was a turning point. As an action and not primarily a research agency, OFDA saw a different "face of the issue" (in Graham Allison's terms) than the others, especially USGS. That is, the *mission* opportunities for OFDA inherent in the Brady-Spence prediction were irresistible. Given that Brady's model was mission enhancing for OFDA but scientifically questionable and organizationally threatening to USGS, the bureaucratic conflict between the two was inevitable. Then the alliances formed: (1) Protecting "one of its own" and rivalrous with USGS, USBM aligned with OFDA, which captured USAID. (2) Disturbed by interagency wrangling that put a loose cannon on the deck of Peruvian-U.S. relations, the State Department sided with USGS. (3) Legitimately fearful of the prediction's implications but also tempted by organizational advantages within in Peru, Giesecke had to tread the fine line between the conflicting U.S. agencies but ended up being perceived as allied with Brady and with OFDA. (4) Also caught in the middle, the U.S. Embassy in Lima attempted to remind U.S. agencies of Peruvian concerns but still represent U.S. policy to the Peruvian government, which made them few friends on either side.

Organizational and personal stakes in the dispute were then raised dramatically by media coverage of the prediction. Late in 1979 in Peru and a year later in the U.S., media attention made the Brady-Spence prediction a public, not merely a governmental, issue. By expanding the real and potential arena, media attention sharpened *all* of the conflicts both within and between the Peruvian and U.S. governments. The year difference in media attention between Peru and the U.S. made matters especially difficult for the U.S. Embassy in Lima. Embassy and USAID personnel in Lima had to confront a public issue in Peru while dealing with Washington agencies that still saw the prediction as "contained." Thus, not only was the problem differently perceived in Lima and Washington, but very different cost-benefit calculations were assigned to each policy option.

Finally, the earthquake prediction establishment did not attack Brady and Spence until the NEPEC meeting, precisely because the basic scientific understanding of earthquakes is incomplete. With USGS somewhat divided between Golden and Menlo Park, and the broader scientific community still groping for an encompassing theory which would allow a true technology of prediction to be developed, Brady and Spence had considerable "space" in which to develop the prediction for Peru.

In sum, given (1) the highly competitive nature of funded research, (2) a race to fill out a paradigm with tremendous lifesaving potential, (3) international, inter-agency, and intra-agency differences, and (4) media coverage, it is small wonder that the Brady-Spence controversy persisted and became so "political."

In closing, we should note that earthquake prediction is an emergent capability, and given the global framework of the plate tectonic approach, other international predictions are inevitable. It appears that none will follow the path of the Brady-Spence prediction, however. By its very existence, the controversy has affected the way subsequent predictions have been and will be handled, convincing scientists to stay quiet and announce predictions only after the fact.

NOTES

Chapter One

1. Thomas S. Kuhn, *The Structure of Scientific Revolutions* (Chicago: University of Chicago Press, 1962).

2. Ibid., 2d ed. (Chicago: University of Chicago Press, 1970), p. 189 (italics in the original).

3. Nathan Reingold, "Through Paradigm-Land to a Normal History of Science," *Social Studies of Science 10* (1980), p. 480.

4. Kuhn, *The Structure*, 2d ed., pp. 209–210 (emphasis added).

5. Don K. Price, *Government and Science* (New York: New York University Press, 1954), and *The Scientific Estate* (Cambridge: Harvard University Press, 1965); Robert Gilpin and Christopher Wright (eds.), *Scientists and National Policy-Making* (New York: Columbia University Press, 1964); Stuart S. Blume, *Toward a Political Sociology of Science* (New York: Free Press, 1974); W. Henry Lambright, *Governing Science and Technology* (New York: Oxford University Press, 1976); and David Dickson, *The New Politics of Science* (New York: Pantheon, 1984).

6. Daniel A. Greenberg, *The Politics of Pure Science* (New York: New American Library, 1967), and Marlan Blissett, *Politics in Science* (Boston: Little, Brown, 1972).

7. Blissett, *Politics in Science*, p. 93.

8. Ibid., pp. 93–94.

9. Ibid., p. 118.

10. Ibid., p. 132.

11. An optimistic early assessment of an "imminent" earthquake prediction capability was Frank Press, "Earthquake Prediction," *Scientific American 232* (May 1975), pp. 14–23. A more chastened update is Robert C. Wesson and Robert C. Wallace, "Predicting the Next Great Earthquake in California," *Scientific American 252* (February 1985), pp. 35–43.

Chapter Two

1. National Research Council Panel on the Public Policy Implications of Earthquake Prediction, *Earthquake Prediction and Public Policy* (Washington, D.C.: National Academy of Sciences, 1975), p. 24 (italics in the original).

2. National Research Council Committee on Socioeconomic Effects of Earthquake Predictions, *A Program of Studies on the Socioeconomic Effects of Earthquake Predictions* (Washington, D.C.: National Academy of Sciences, 1978), p. 1.

3. Luther Carter, "Earthquake Prediction: ESSA and USGS Vie for Leadership," *Science 151* (January 14, 1966), p. 181. See also W. Henry Lambright, "Policymaking for Earthquake Prediction in America and Japan," Third U.S.-Japan Seminar on Science Policy, Honolulu,. Hawaii, February 19–23, 1983.

4. The *Pure and Applied Geophysics* articles were as follows: B. T. Brady, "Theory of Earthquakes I: A Scale Independent Theory of Rock Failure," *112* (1974), pp. 701–725; "Theory of Earthquakes II: Inclusion Theory of Crustal Earthquakes," *113* (1975), pp. 149–167; "Theory of

Earthquakes III: Inclusion Collapse Theory of Deep Earthquakes," *114* (1976), pp. 119–139; "Theory of Earthquakes IV: General Implications for Earthquake Prediction," *114* (1976), pp. 1031–1082.

5. Brady, "Theory of Earthquakes IV," p. 1067.

6. Ibid., p. 1069.

7. "Conference Report: Toward Earthquake Prediction on the Global Scale," *EOS 59* (January 1978), p. 40.

8. For an assessment of various facets of the Peruvian revolutionary period and its aftermath, see Stephen M. Gorman (ed.), *Post-Revolutionary Peru: The Politics of Transformation* (Boulder, Colo.: Westview, 1982).

9. Internal USBM memo from Brian Brady (Denver) to Robert Marovelli (Washington), June 5, 1978.

10. Letter from Brian Brady (USBM–Denver) to Enrique Silgado (CERESIS–Lima), January 11, 1977. We should explain here that typographical errors and misspellings are numerous in these documents. To facilitate understanding we have corrected all obvious mistakes.

11. Memo from Brian Brady (USBM–Denver) to L. C. Pakiser (USGS–Golden), August 25, 1977 (emphasis added).

12. See Alberto A. Giesecke, "Case History of the Peru Prediction for 1980–81," *Proceedings of the Seminar on Earthquake Prediction Case Histories* (Geneva: UNDRO, 1983), p. 60.

13. Field Message 004 from USICA–Lima to USICA–Washington, April 10, 1978.

14. Ibid.

15. Ibid. (emphasis added).

16. Internal USBM memo from Brian Brady (Denver) to Robert Marovelli (Washington), June 5, 1978.

17. Ibid. (emphasis added).

18. Ibid.

19. Ibid. The consensus is that a prediction should

specify the location, magnitude, lead time, time window, and probability of an earthquake. Given that Brady's model was "deterministic" and therefore not qualifiable by probability, it met all the usual conditions.

20. Ibid.

21. Internal USGS memo from Ted Algermissen, Jim Jordan, Lou Pakiser, and Bill Spence (Golden) to Rob Wesson (Reston), January 30, 1979 (emphasis added).

22. Minutes, U.S. Department of Interior (Bureau of Mines recording) Eighteenth Meeting, Geological Survey—Bureau of Mines Coordinating Committee, May 9, 1978.

23. *Christian Science Monitor*, May 10, 1978.

24. Masakazu Ohtake, Tosimatu Matumoto, and Gary V. Latham, "Seismicity Gap near Oaxaca, Southern Mexico as a Probable Precursor to a Large Earthquake," *Pure and Applied Geophysics 115* (1977), pp. 375–385. It should be noted that this same journal published the Brady series.

25. Letter from Alberto Giesecke (IGP–Lima) to H. William Menard (director, USGS–Reston), January 19, 1979.

26. Internal USGS memo cited in note 21.

27. Letter from USGS Acting Director James R. Basley to Alberto Giesecke (IGP–Lima), February 1, 1979.

28. Letter from Assistant Secretary of State for Inter-American Affairs Viron P. Vaky to USBM Director Roger Markle, February 9, 1979.

29. Letter from USBM Director Roger Markle to Assistant Secretary of State for Inter-American Affairs Viron P. Vaky, February 27, 1979.

Chapter Three

1. Internal USGS "Distribution" memo from John Filson (USGS–Reston), May 2, 1979.

2. Internal USBM memo from Brian Brady (Denver) to Robert Marovelli (Washington), June 19, 1979 (emphasis in the original).

3. Internal OFDA memo from Paul Krumpe to OFDA Director Anne Martindell, June 19, 1979.

4. Internal USGS memo from Bill Spence (Golden) to Bob Engdahl (Golden), Jerry Eaton (Menlo Park), "and others," August 1, 1979 (emphasis in the original).

5. "Prospectus for an Earthquake Prediction Program," from John Derr (USGS–Golden) to USGS–Reston, undated.

6. Draft letter from Brian Brady (USBM–Denver) and Bill Spence (USGS–Golden) to Alberto Giesecke (IGP–Lima), October 26, 1979.

7. Ibid.

8. Internal OFDA memo from Paul Krumpe to W. R. Dalton, November 13, 1979.

9. Alberto A. Giesecke, "Case History of the Peru Prediction for 1980–81," *Proceedings of the Seminar on Earthquake Prediction Case Histories* (Geneva: UNDRO, 1983), p. 60.

10. U.S. Embassy–Lima cable ("Lima 00090") to secretary of state, January 4, 1980.

11. Ibid.

12. Ibid.

13. Ibid.

14. Letter from Rob Wesson (USGS–Reston) to W. R. Dalton (OFDA), January 8, 1980.

15. Ibid.

16. Letter from W. R. Dalton (OFDA) to Rob Wesson (USGS–Reston), January 15, 1980 (emphasis added).

17. Letter from Robert Marovelli (USBM–Washington) to W. R. Dalton (OFDA), February 22, 1980 (emphasis added).

18. Letter from Alberto Giesecke (CERESIS–Lima) to Jim Jordan (USGS–Golden), January 20, 1980.

Chapter Four

1. FEMA internal memo from Director of International Affairs Frederick Ackerson to FEMA Director John Macy, February 13, 1980.

2. Ibid.

3. Translated from Alberto A. Giesecke, "Algunos Aspectos de la Reacción ante la Predicción de un Terremoto en el Peru," *Revista Geofísica 13* (Mexico, July–December 1980), p. 47. Written while the case was still unfolding, this four-page piece is at least as important as Giesecke's subsequent "Case History of the Peru Prediction for 1980–81," *Proceedings of the Seminar on Earthquake Prediction Case Histories* (Geneva: UNDRO, 1983), pp. 51–75. Leonidas Ocola also notes that the stated goal for increased IGP funding was to create "an earthquake prediction program at the national level," in his *Informe, Predicción Sísmica en el Peru: Parametros Importantes, Programa General, y Equipamiento* (Lima: IGP, April 1980, mimeo), p. 1.

4. Giesecke, "Case History of the Peru Prediction," p. 61.

5. U.S. Embassy–Lima cable ("Lima 1782") to secretary of state, February 29, 1980.

6. Ibid.

7. Ibid.

8. Letter from Brian Brady (USBM–Denver) to Rob Wesson (USGS–Reston), March 7, 1980 (emphasis added). A separate story lies behind this letter. On March 3, 1980, Brady wrote a longer letter in the same vein addressed to W. R. Dalton at OFDA. It was never sent, however. According to a handwritten note by Chi-shing Wang on the cover page, "This letter was never issued. It was revised and addressed to Bob Wesson, USGS, instead of Dalton, AID." Deleted from the original version to be sent to Dalton was the following paragraph:

I am sure you are aware that a divergence of opinion exists between myself and OES [USGS Office of Earthquake Studies] on the credibility of my theory and its relationship to the Peru prediction. Yet, while OES is considered to be the expert on the earthquake prediction problem, I must pose three questions for your examination. *First*, why has OES not predicted, even forecast one earthquake within or outside the continental United States? The current rash of large events in northern and southern California [August 6, 1979—Coyote Lake event, M = 5.9; October 15, 1979—El Centro event, M = 6.8; January 24, 1980, and January 27, 1980—Livermore events, M = 5.5 and 5.8, respectively, and the February 25, 1980, M = 5.1 event along the San Jacinto fault system] appears to have surprised OES. *Second*, if a scientist not associated with OES successfully forecasted the El Centro event, why has there been no attempt by OES scientists to inquire how the forecast was made? Why has there been no transmittal of seismic data preceding and immediately following this event? *Third*, if OES generally accepts the seismic gap paradigm, why has OES refused to acknowledge the possibilities of instrumenting and studying the large gap in Peru discussed by Spence in a country friendly to the United States?

9. OFDA internal memo from W. R. Dalton to OFDA Director Joseph A. Mitchell, March 28, 1980.

10. Internal USBM–Washington memo from Chi-shing Wang to Robert Marovelli, March 27, 1980.

11. Ibid.

12. OFDA internal memo from "Senior Planning Officer" Weston Emery to W. R. Dalton, April 1, 1980.

13. OFDA internal memo from "Joyce" to W. R. Dalton, April 3, 1980.

14. Letter from USGS–Reston Director H. William Menard to Frank Press, director, Office of Science and Technology Policy, May 6, 1980.

15. Internal USGS memo from John Filson to "Chief, Global Seismology Branch," May 27, 1980.

16. Handwritten note of telephone conversation by Chi-shing Wang of April 15, 1980, confirmed at the foot of internal USBM memo from R. O. Swenarton (chief, Office of Public Information) to Brian Brady, April 16, 1980.

17. "Earthquake Risk and Preparedness in Peru, with Special Reference to the Predictions for 1981–1982" (Geneva: UNDRO, June 10, 1980, mimeo), p. 1.

18. Ibid., p. 4.

19. Ibid., pp. 8–9.

20. Ibid., p. 9.

21. Ibid.

22. Ibid., p. 11.

23. Ibid.

24. Letter from Alberto Giesecke (chief, IGP) to Leonard Yaeger (director, USAID–Lima), June 10, 1980.

25. Ibid.

26. Department of State cable ("State 188396") to U.S. Embassy–Lima, July 17, 1980.

27. Ibid.

28. Ibid.

29. Giesecke, "Case History of the Peru Prediction," p. 62.

30. U.S. Embassy–Lima cable ("Lima 7023") to secretary of state, August 6, 1980.

31. "Report to the Agency for International Development on a Trip to Peru from Aug 17 to Sept 1, 1980 by Jerry P. Eaton, Geophysicist of the United States Geological Survey" (mimeo, undated).

32. Ibid.

33. U.S. Embassy–Lima cable ("Lima 8389") to secretary of state, September 15, 1980.

34. John Tomblin, "Report on Disaster Preparedness Mission to Peru" (Geneva: UNDRO, October 6–14, 1980, mimeo), p. 1.

35. Ibid., p. 8 (or p. 1 of "annex").

36. Department of State cable ("State 277382") to U.S. Embassy–Lima and U.S. Embassy–Buenos Aires, October 17, 1980 (emphasis added).

37. Ibid. (emphasis added).

38. Ibid.

39. National Earthquake Prediction Evaluation Council, "Minutes of the Meeting, February 4–5, 1980," USGS–Reston.

40. USAID internal memo from Fred Cole and Paul Krumpe (OFDA) to "The Director, USAID/Peru," November 2 (approximate date), 1980.

41. U.S. Embassy–Lima cable ("Lima 10336") to secretary of state, November 10, 1980.

42. Ibid.

43. Internal OFDA memo from Paul Krumpe and Fred Cole to Alan Van Egmond, November 12, 1980.

44. Ibid. (emphasis added).

45. Internal USGS memo from E. R. Engdahl, chief, Branch of Global Seismology, to John Filson, acting chief, Office of Earthquake Studies, November 3, 1980.

46. Internal OFDA memo from Paul Krumpe and Fred Cole to Alan Van Egmond, November 12, 1980.

Chapter Five

1. A corroborating description may be found in "Future Shock: New Theory Predicts a Violent Earthquake for Peru Next August," *Discover* 2 (January 1981), p. 61.

2. Internal OFDA memo from Paul Krumpe to Alan Van Egmond, November 18, 1980 (emphasis in the original).

3. Ibid.

4. Ibid.

5. Internal OFDA memo from Alan Van Egmond to OFDA Director Joseph Mitchell, November 18, 1980.

6. Memo of conversation of November 19, 1980, between Gordon Pierson (USAID), Edward Coy (USAID), Alan Van Egmond (OFDA), Robert Wesson (USGS–Reston), and John Filson (USGS–Reston), prepared by Van Egmond, November 25, 1980.

7. Ibid.

8. Ibid.

9. Ibid.

10. Memo of conversation of November 21, 1980, between John Filson (USGS–Reston) and Ollie Davidson (OFDA), prepared by Davidson, November 21, 1980.

11. Internal USGS–Reston memo from Roger Stewart, "Deputy for Research," to "Chief, Office of Earthquake Studies," November 21, 1980.

12. Ibid.

13. U.S. Embassy–Lima cable ("Lima 10984") to secretary of state, December 2, 1980.

14. Ibid.

15. U.S. Embassy–Lima cable ("Lima 10889") to secretary of state, November 28, 1980.

16. Ibid.

17. Department of State cable ("State 324986") to U.S. Embassy–Lima, December 8, 1980.

18. *Science 200* (June 1978), p. 434.

Chapter Six

1. *Charter, National Earthquake Prediction Evaluation Council* (Reston, Va.: USGS, 1979).

2. Ibid.

3. Brian T. Brady, "Anomalous Seismicity prior to Rock Bursts: Implications for Earthquake Prediction," *Pure and Applied Geophysics 115* (1977), pp. 357–374.

4. Letter from Robert L. Wesson, for Director H. William Menard (USGS–Reston), to Director Roger Markle (USBM–Washington), January 13, 1981.

5. Chi-shing Wang's handwritten notes on "Telephone Conversation with John Filson USGS—(Brady's Trial)—January 12, 1981 4:00 P.M."

6. Ibid.

7. Internal USBM memo from Donald C. Rogich, director, Division of Research Center Operations (Washington) to research director, Denver Research Center, January 15, 1981.

8. Internal OFDA memo from Paul Krumpe to Alan Van Egmond, December 21, 1980 (emphasis added).

9. Internal USAID/OFDA memo from Ron Nicholson to Alan Van Egmond, January 23, 1981.

10. Ibid.

11. Personal interview with John Filson, USGS–Reston, August 26, 1983.

12. Internal USAID/OFDA memo from Ron Nicholson to Alan Van Egmond, January 23, 1981.

13. U.S. Embassy–Lima cable ("Lima 906") to secretary of state, January 27, 1981.

14. *Charter, National Earthquake Prediction Evaluation Council.*

15. Department of Interior, Transcript of Proceedings, *In the Matter of: The National Earthquake Prediction Evaluation Council Meeting to Receive Evidence and to Assess the Validity of a Prediction Calling for a Great Earthquake off the Coat [sic] of Peru in August 1981* (Reston, Va.: USGS, 1981), pp. 10–11. There are two peculiar aspects to this 347-page transcript. First, it is very difficult to obtain. Paul Krumpe has stated that he tried to secure a copy,

but was unsuccessful. Our copy comes from the Office of the Director at USGS–Reston and is, we believe, the only copy outside USGS. The second peculiarity is the total lack of editing. Typographical errors are legion; spelling is atrocious; punctuation is almost totally lacking; and inappropriate words are used (for example, when "deformation," a geologic term, is clearly intended by the speaker, "defamation," a courtroom term, is used). Therefore, in the quotations drawn from the transcript, we have tried to improve the readability and clean up at least the most glaring errors.

16. Ibid., p. 11.

17. Ibid., pp. 8–9.

18. Ibid., p. 14.

19. Ibid., p. 70. To illustrate the transcript problem, the original states "Einstein's Fuel Equation."

20. Ibid., pp. 71–74.

21. Ibid., pp. 74–75.

22. Ibid.

23. Ibid., p. 90.

24. Ibid., pp. 90–91.

25. Ibid., p. 95.

26. Ibid., p. 118.

27. Ibid., pp. 108–142, especially pp. 128–142.

28. Ibid., p. 150.

29. Ibid., pp. 155–156.

30. Ibid., p. 159.

31. Ibid., p. 180.

32. Ibid., pp. 180–181 (emphases added).

33. Ibid., p. 184.

34. Ibid., p. 221.

35. Ibid., p. 224.

36. Ibid., pp. 232–233.

37. Ibid., pp. 233–234.

38. Ibid., p. 236.

39. Ibid.
40. Ibid., p. 237.
41. Ibid., p. 238.

Chapter Seven

1. Department of Interior, Transcript of Proceedings, *In the Matter of: The National Earthquake Prediction Evaluation Council Meeting to Receive Evidence and to Assess the Validity of a Prediction Calling for a Great Earthquake off the Coat* [*sic*] *of Peru in August 1981* (Reston, Va.: USGS, 1981), p. 239.
2. Ibid., pp. 240–243.
3. Ibid., p. 244.
4. Ibid., p. 245.
5. Ibid., pp. 246–247.
6. Ibid., p. 250.
7. Ibid., pp. 251–252.
8. Ibid., p. 252.
9. Ibid., pp. 258–259.
10. Ibid., p. 263.
11. Ibid., pp. 264–266.
12. Ibid., p. 267.
13. Ibid., p. 268.
14. Ibid.
15. Ibid., pp. 268–270 (emphases added).
16. Ibid., pp. 270–271.
17. Ibid., p. 272.
18. Ibid.
19. Ibid., p. 283.
20. Ibid., p. 286.
21. Ibid.
22. Ibid., p. 325.
23. Ibid., pp. 328–330.
24. Ibid., pp. 338–340.

25. Ibid., pp. 340–341.

26. Ibid., pp. 346–347.

27. *Statement, National Earthquake Prediction Evaluation Council*, January 27, 1981 (Reston, Va.: USGS, 1981).

28. Richard Kerr, "Prediction of Huge Peruvian Quakes Quashed," *Science 211* (February 20, 1981), p. 809.

29. Ibid.

Chapter Eight

1. Jean-Paul Levy (UNDRO), Oliver Davidson (OFDA), Jose Bravo (FEMA), Paul Flores (San Diego County, California), Douglas Zischke (private consultant), Enrique Massafero (Pan American Health Organization), Jose Luis Zeballos (Pan American Health Organization), and Alejandro James (League of Red Cross Societies), "Disaster Preparedness and Prevention in Peru" (Geneva: UNDRO, January 31, 1981, mimeo), p. 1.

2. Ibid., p. 3.

3. Ibid., p. 4.

4. Ibid., p. 20.

5. Telephone interview, January 23, 1984.

6. Electronic Memo #16, R. Evans (USGS–Denver) to "GS Management," January 29, 1981.

7. Ibid.

8. Internal USBM memo from Brian Brady (Denver) to Robert Marovelli (Washington), February 12, 1981.

9. Transcript of "Quakecast" on *Walter Cronkite's Universe*, Volume I, Number 2, June 23, 1981, as broadcast over the CBS Television Network.

10. "Telephone Conversation, Waddell, Brady, Hooker, Marovelli, Wang," by Chi-shing Wang, January 23, 1981.

11. "Telephone Conversation with B. Brady," by Chishing Wang, February 5, 1981.

12. Internal OFDA memo from Paul Krumpe to Alan Van Egmond, February 6, 1981.

13. Ibid. (emphasis added).

14. Ibid.

15. Ibid.

16. Internal OFDA memo from Alan Van Egmond to OFDA Director Joseph A. Mitchell, February 4, 1981.

17. Ibid.

18. Internal USAID information memorandum from Gordon Pierson to USAID Acting Administrator M. Peter McPherson, February 19, 1981.

19. Internal USAID memo from M. Peter McPherson to Gordon Pierson, March 9, 1981.

20. Internal OFDA memo from Paul Krumpe to Alan Van Egmond, March 24, 1981.

21. Internal USAID memo from Gordon Pierson to M. Peter McPherson, March 25, 1981. The internal quotation is from the NEPEC statement of January 27, 1981, itself.

22. Ibid.

23. Ibid.

24. Internal OFDA memo from Paul Krumpe to OFDA Director Martin Howell, April 22, 1981.

25. U.S. Embassy–Lima cable ("Lima 4135") to secretary of state, April 23, 1981.

26. Letter from Brian Brady (USBM–Denver) to Alberto Giesecke (CERESIS–Lima), April 28, 1981 (emphasis in the original).

27. Letter from Alberto Giesecke (CERESIS–Lima) to Roger Guerra–Garcia (president, Consejo Nacional de Investigación), Lima, April 2, 1981. Giesecke cited John Roberts, "Political and Administrative Considerations in

the Establishment of an Earthquake Prediction and Warning Procedure," *Revista Geofísica 13* (Mexico, July–December 1980), pp. 25–35.

28. Letter from Ramon Cabré (president, Consejo Directivo of CERESIS) to Roger Guerra-Garcia, May 18, 1981.

29. Ibid.

30. Letter from Roger Guerra-Garcia (president, Consejo Nacional de Investigación) to President of Peru Fernando Belaúnde Terry, May 22, 1981.

31. Internal USBM memo from Brian Brady (Denver) to Robert Marovelli (Washington), May 7, 1981.

32. Ibid. (emphasis in the original).

33. Ibid. (emphasis in the original).

34. Internal OFDA memo from Paul Krumpe to OFDA Director Martin Howell, May 8, 1981.

35. Ibid.

36. Memo from USAID Administrator M. Peter McPherson to Secretary of State Alexander Haig, prepared by OFDA Director Martin Howell, draft date May 14, 1981.

Chapter Nine

1. U.S. Embassy–Lima cable ("Lima 5079") to secretary of state, May 21, 1981.

2. These are drawn from (1) Paul J. Flores, "Final Report, Contract PDC-0012-5-00-1052-00," submitted to OFDA in August 1981, and (2) personal interviews conducted in Los Angeles, California, and Tempe, Arizona, in 1982 and 1983.

3. Flores, "Final Report," p. 5.

4. Ibid., p. 10.

5. U.S. Embassy–Lima cable ("Lima 5658") to secretary of state, June 8, 1981.

6. Ibid.

7. Internal USGS memo from William Spence (Golden) to John Filson (Reston), June 10, 1981.

8. Ibid.

9. Internal OFDA memo from Paul Krumpe to OFDA Director Martin Howell, June 12, 1981 (emphasis in the original).

10. Internal USBM memo from Brian Brady (Denver) to Donald Rogich (Washington), June 19, 1981.

11. Ibid.

12. Memo from Edward Coy (USAID–Latin America) to OFDA Director Martin Howell, June 22, 1981.

13. Letter from J. Andrew Purnell (U.S. Consulate, Poznan, Poland) to Richard Stuart Olson, December 27, 1983.

14. Ibid.

15. Internal OFDA memo from Paul Krumpe to Alan Van Egmond, June 24, 1981 (emphasis added).

16. Ibid.

17. Letter to Richard Stuart Olson, December 27, 1983 (emphasis added).

18. U.S. Embassy–Lima cable ("Lima 6427") to secretary of state, July 2, 1981. One of the few humorous anecdotes to come out of this entire affair occurred at this time. U.S. Ambassador Edwin Corr was coincidentally bringing his mother and father to Lima in mid-June. Reporters happened to see him at the airport waiting for his parents and asked him what he was doing there. Jokingly, Corr said that he was bringing his mother to Peru and would "stake her on the beach" to await the supposed tsunami. The media reported the statement as straight news. President Belaúnde and several members

of the cabinet called Corr personally to congratulate him on this brilliant tactic! Our interview notes fail to indicate whether the senior Mrs. Corr was amused.

19. Internal USGS "trip report" from John Filson (Reston) to "Chief Geologist" (Reston), July 9, 1981.

20. Ibid.

21. Ibid.

22. Draft letter from Brian Brady (USBM–Denver) to Alberto Giesecke (CERESIS–Lima), July 9, 1981.

23. Letter from USBM deputy director to Dallas Peck, chief geologist, USGS–Reston, July 29, 1981.

24. Letter from Clarence Allen (California Institute of Technology) to USAID Administrator M. Peter McPherson, July 10, 1981.

25. Ibid.

26. Ibid.

27. Ibid.

28. Letter from OFDA Director Martin Howell to Clarence Allen (California Institute of Technology), July 22, 1981. Known informally as "Tiger" Howell, this retired military officer believed (according to a close observer) that "when men under your command are attacked, you protect them."

29. Ibid.

30. Letter from Alberto Giesecke (CERESIS–Lima) to OFDA Director Martin Howell, January 11, 1982.

31. Letter from John Filson (USGS–Reston) to Alberto Giesecke (CERESIS–Lima), January 5, 1982.

INDEX

Several individuals appear so often throughout this book that complete citation would defeat the purpose of indexing. Especially for Brian Brady, William Spence, Alberto Giesecke, Paul Krumpe, and John Filson, we have been selective with page references, attempting to hit only the "high points" (key events, positions taken, important memos, and so on). It turns out that a drama does not index easily.

185

187